ORTHO® ALL ABOUT

Sprinklers
& Drip Systems

Meredith® Books
Des Moines, Iowa

All About Sprinklers & Drip Systems

Editor: Benjamin W. Allen
Copy Chief: Terri Fredrickson
Publishing Operations Manager: Karen Schirm
Senior Editor, Asset and Information Manager:
  Phillip Morgan
Edit and Design Production Coordinator: Mary Lee Gavin
Editorial and Design Assistant: Kathleen Stevens
Book Production Managers: Pam Kvitne,
  Marjorie J. Schenkelberg, Rick von Holdt, Mark Weaver
Contributing Copy Editor: Patricia Ingraham
Technical Proofreader: Michael D. Smith
Contributing Proofreaders: Pam Elizian, Sara Henderson,
  Jodie Littleton
Contributing Map Illustrator: Jana Fothergill
Indexer: Deborah Dillon

Additional Editorial Contributions from Greenleaf Publishing, Inc.

Project Editor: Dave Toht
Copy Editor: Barbara Webb
Editorial Assistant: Deborah Dillon
Graphic Design: Rebecca Anderson
Illustrators: Rebecca Anderson, Tony Davis, Mike Grundy

Thanks to: Autumn Skies Landscapes; Central Valley Builders Supply; Deborah Cowder; Darco, Inc.; Malia Landis; David and Joy Long; George and Connie Zieseimer; Orbit Irrigation Products Inc.; The Toro Company; Anthony Torres; The Urban Farmer Store; David Van Ness

Meredith® Books

Executive Director, Editorial: Gregory H. Kayko
Executive Director, Design: Matt Strelecki
Managing Editor: Amy Tincher-Durik
Executive Editor/Group Manager: Benjamin W. Allen
Senior Associate Design Director: Tom Wegner
Marketing Product Manager: Isaac Petersen

Publisher and Editor in Chief: James D. Blume
Editorial Director: Linda Raglan Cunningham
Executive Director, New Business Development:
  Todd M. Davis
Executive Director, Sales: Ken Zagor
Director, Operations: George A. Susral
Director, Production: Douglas M. Johnston
Director, Marketing: Amy Nichols
Business Director: Jim Leonard

Vice President and General Manager: Douglas J. Guendel

Meredith Publishing Group

President: Jack Griffin
Executive Vice President: Bob Mate

Meredith Corporation

Chairman and Chief Executive Officer: William T. Kerr
President and Chief Operating Officer: Stephen M. Lacy

In Memoriam: E.T. Meredith III (1933–2003)

Photographers:
(Photographers credited may retain copyright © to the listed photographs.)
L = Left, R = Right, B = Bottom, T = Top

Gay Bumgarner: 26
Pat Bruno, Positive Images: 6R
Josephine Coatsworth: 70, 113T
Crandall & Crandall: 112
Derek Fell: 11
Greenleaf Publishing: Back cover, 7, 8, 12, 19, 24T, 30, 31, 33T, 36, 40T, 44T, 44B, 49B, 72T, 75B, 77T, 92, 108, 115T, 115B
Saxon Holt: 15
Michael Landis: Cover, 1, 6L, 17, 28, 34, 40-41, 42, 44C, 46, 47, 49T, 76, 94-95, 100, 113B
Charles Mann: 21
Orbit® Irrigation Products Inc.: 48, 77B, 98T
The Scotts Miracle-Gro Company: 33B, 78
Graeme Teague: 72-73
The Toro Company: Back cover, 27, 29B, 32, 45, 75T, 83, 98BL, 98BR, 99, 101, 103

Cover photograph: Michael Landis

All of us at Meredith® Books are dedicated to providing you with the information and ideas you need to enhance your home and garden. We welcome your comments and suggestions about this book. Write to us at:
  Meredith Corporation
  Meredith Gardening Books
  1716 Locust St.
  Des Moines, IA 50309–3023

If you would like more information on other Ortho products, call 800/225-2883 or visit us at: www.ortho.com

Note to the Readers: Due to differing conditions, tools, and individual skills, Meredith Corporation assumes no responsibility for any damages, injuries suffered, or losses incurred as a result of following the information published in this book. Before beginning any project, review the instructions carefully, and if any doubts or questions remain, consult local experts or authorities. Because codes and regulations vary greatly, you always should check with authorities to ensure that your project complies with all applicable local codes and regulations. Always read and observe all of the safety precautions provided by manufacturers of any tools, equipment, or supplies, and follow all accepted safety procedures.

Contents

IRRIGATION BASICS

If you spend too much time watering, or if your lawn, garden, and shrubs sometimes get less water than they require, adding a home irrigation system may be the solution. Home irrigation systems are reliable and nearly invisible, and they often pay for themselves. But irrigation isn't for every yard or garden; read this chapter to decide if it's for yours.

A well-planned irrigation system is cost-effective, unobtrusive, and durable. An automatic system will make your life a bit easier. A properly installed irrigation system will supply the correct amount of water to the intended place, so your plants and lawn will be thoroughly fed without wasting water.

When planning your irrigation system, consider not only your climate but also the microclimates on your property caused by varying amounts of shade, slope, and wind. Also factor in the type of soil you have. Plan your landscaping along with your irrigation system for the best results over the long term.

▼ **A properly planned irrigation system makes it easy to keep your landscape in tip-top shape.**

THE ADVANTAGES OF HOME IRRIGATION

Landscaping not only beautifies your home, it also increases its value. Anything that helps you maintain your landscaping in better condition is worth considering. This means that irrigation may be one of the best home investments you can make.

Healthy, green gardens

There are no two ways about it: Plants grow best when all their watering needs are met in a timely manner. Haphazard, irregular watering results in patchy, uneven growth. Compare the yards in your neighborhood that are irrigated with those that are not. This shouldn't be hard; they can usually be distinguished from a distance. The irrigated lawns are generally greener and lusher. Their hedges, trees, and shrubs are denser and less subject to summer yellowing, and their flower gardens grow more quickly and remain in peak bloom longer. Vegetable gardens are much more productive, often yielding twice as much produce per square foot as do nonirrigated gardens, and the vegetables are often larger, better formed, tastier, and earlier to mature.

Proper irrigation also results in healthier plants. Plants that are watered irregularly develop smaller root systems, grow more slowly, and are more susceptible to insects, disease, and cold damage than those that receive even watering. Many insects are actually attracted to wilted, yellowing leaves. Irregular hose watering can splash leaves with contaminated soil, spreading many bacterial and fungal diseases.

▼ **Irregular watering leads to increased insect problems, yellowed leaves, and weak, patchy growth.**

Properly planned irrigation can direct water at root level and can be timed to coincide with the drying effect of the sun, which can lessen disease spread.

Practicality and convenience

Of course you can water by hand and save the expense of irrigation, but are you always around at the right time? And do you always have the time? Running around the yard moving hoses and sprinklers is not always fun, and local restrictions that may limit watering to impossible hours of the night make hand watering even less appealing. That's why irrigation systems are so practical. With the use of a timer, it is possible to set the system to start when you are asleep or at work. You can even program your system to come on regularly while you are away on vacation.

■ **Easy installation:** Any irrigation system is going to take some installation, but techniques have improved and been simplified greatly since home irrigation first became readily available after World War II. The old-fashioned metal-pipe systems were unwieldy and complicated to install and required soldering, specialized equipment, and considerable skill.

▲ **Once installed, an irrigation system will blend in with the landscape and become nearly invisible.**

▲ **Hand watering can be messy and time-consuming, and wastes water.**

Modern watering systems make installation easy, with piping and heads that simply snap or glue together, and tubing that is cut easily to appropriate lengths. It is now not only feasible but relatively easy to install a modest system in a couple of weekends, especially if the irrigation plans have been carefully prepared. Most irrigation suppliers offer a wide range of products to meet almost every need.

You can also rent trenching equipment that makes the most laborious part of installation, digging the holes, almost easy. The equipment causes so little damage to the lawn that, within only a week, you can barely see any evidence of the digging.

Cost-effectiveness: The major concern of any homeowner considering installing an irrigation system used to be the cost. The arrival of new lightweight materials has changed all that, bringing the cost of installing a system within the reach of just about every budget. Although prices vary widely according to the size of the property and its particular needs, many homeowners find that an efficient irrigation system can usually be installed for less than $5,000 and often for less than $3,000. Most systems will pay for themselves in only a few years through improved growth of lawn and garden, reduced loss of plants to drought, and greatly decreased yard maintenance. Furthermore, irrigation increases the value of your property; the presence of an effective irrigation system can make a major difference in its salability.

Tailor-made: Lawn and garden irrigation can be tailored to your specific needs. Hose-driven sprinklers water everything haphazardly, overwatering slopes and leaving dry pockets behind shrubs and trees. Irrigation, on the other hand, can be extremely efficient. Different *zones* (sometimes referred to as *circuits*) with watering periods that vary in both frequency and duration ensure each planting gets the water it needs, when it needs it. And you can plan the system so it waters just the lawns and gardens, not the sidewalks, windows, and streets.

You can also match the level of control to your needs: An irrigation system can be almost entirely automated, completely manual, or anywhere in between. Because landscape plantings grow and change over time, watering requirements will also change—and modern irrigation systems are easily adaptable. Sprayer heads can be adjusted or changed, and systems using sprinklers and bubblers can be converted to systems using drip irrigation or microsprinklers. It is also a relatively easy matter to add new sprayer heads to an existing system, as long as some space is left for future expansion during the initial planning.

Nearly invisible: You can barely see a well-planned irrigation system—it is nearly invisible. Underground pipes and discreetly placed sprayers or drippers blend into the landscape. Some sprinklers even pop up to water, then disappear underground when their job is done. Compare that with the look of a hand-watered landscape: tangled hoses in dangerous array all over the yard.

■ **Built to last:** Modern irrigation systems are composed mostly of weather-resistant plastic products, which are not subject to rust or decomposition. They can be expected to last twenty years or more, and some carry lifetime guarantees on product workmanship. Individual parts—such as sprinkler heads—that are exposed to damage from passing feet, flying footballs, and lawn mowers can be adjusted or replaced easily. In fact the only routine maintenance needed in most climates is annual draining, occasional cleaning of exposed parts, and, in the case of drip systems, regular flushing to prevent the buildup of deposits. If even that small amount of maintenance sounds like too much, you can contract out the maintenance to a specialist for a modest fee.

■ **Low-maintenance gardening:** As many homeowners do, you may dream of a beautiful landscape that takes care of itself. An irrigation system brings you several steps closer to this goal. If you are looking for maximum upkeep for minimal effort, you will want to automate the system to the utmost. See page 98. The use of a water sensor or rain gauge, in addition to the basic timer, means the system will require the least possible human intervention. If you are looking for a less automated system—perhaps because you are a weekend gardener and you want a more hands-on approach—you might prefer an entirely manual system or a semiautomatic one. See page 96.

■ **Low-maintenance cover-ups:** Irrigation is well suited to a process that is central to low-maintenance gardening—mulching. By covering the surface of the soil, mulch prevents weed germination, keeps the ground cooler, slows down evaporation, and generally decreases yard upkeep. Mulch is also the perfect cover for the unattractive tubing of many drip systems.

Another low-maintenance cover-up for tubing is living groundcover, such as low-growing, leafy shrubs, vines, and perennials. These plants are used frequently in low-maintenance gardens, under trees, and on slopes to prevent erosion and provide a low-care substitute for heavy-upkeep lawns. Also with adequate, regular irrigation, groundcovers become established more rapidly and are healthier.

Other low-care plants, such as drought-tolerant trees, shrubs, and ornamental vines, combine perfectly with mulch and irrigation to create easy-care landscapes.

▼ **With the proper irrigation system, your landscape will practically water itself, leaving you more time to appreciate it.**

IRRIGATION AND CONSERVATION

Home irrigation not only provides a means of watering yards and gardens without carrying the hose from spot to spot and without getting wet, it also allows you to apply the appropriate amount of water at the best time, thereby conserving resources.

Water, the source of plant life

Water accounts for 60 to 90 percent of the weight of actively growing plants, including those growing in the desert. Plants use water to build leaves, flowers, and fruits; to transport minerals from the roots to the leaves; and to carry energy from the leaves to the roots—all the basic life processes. Plants are, however, wasteful of water. In nondesert plants, especially, most water is neither used for growth nor stored for future use but is given off in the form of water vapor through stomata, or breathing pores. Plants that do not receive adequate rainfall, therefore, quickly use up whatever water is available in the soil. This happens more rapidly under high heat, because plants transpire more quickly and thus lose water more rapidly.

When plants don't have enough water to carry on their normal life processes, their leaves lose their turgidity and wilt. Wilted plants often recover if watered immediately, but some damage has generally been done. The fragile root hairs, through which plants absorb much of their water, must be in constant contact with at least a thin film of water or they will die. When a plant wilts above ground, you can be sure root hairs are dying down below. Each time a plant wilts, more root hairs die, causing the plant's growth to slow down or stop.

Underwatered plants often lose part of their leaves, abort flower buds, or produce deformed, undersized fruits. Hand watering often puts plants through a constant cycle of drought and abundance that, at best, slows their growth and, at worst, can leave them weak and dying. Irrigation, on the other hand, supplies water just before the soil dries out. Properly irrigated plants never lack water and are healthier and more productive.

The correct amount of water: Home irrigation uses piping to carry water from the main source of supply (the water main, a well, or a water tank) to the plants that need it. It can involve sprinklers and bubblers that visibly spray water onto plantings, often over long distances,

Wilted leaves are one sign that roots have been damaged by the lack of water.

or drip emitters that deliver water to your plants drop by drop, practically unseen.

The principal goal of home irrigation is to water the root zones of plants, trees, and lawns in order to compensate for any moisture not provided by the environment. Irrigation is, therefore, most useful during periods of high heat and low rainfall. Not all plants require the same amount of water or the same frequency of irrigation (this is discussed in greater detail in the final chapter); but, in general, an irrigation system should keep all parts of the lawn and garden evenly moist throughout the growing season.

It is, however, important not to go overboard with irrigation. All plants need air at their roots. If the soil remains constantly waterlogged, any air present in the soil is used up and the roots can no longer breathe. As a result the plant eventually rots and dies. It is essential that the soil remain slightly moist at all times or, if it is allowed to become saturated to the point of puddling, that the excess water be allowed to drain thoroughly before the next watering.

Fertilizer needs water: A proper water supply is vital to a plant's mineral intake. Fertilizer is usually applied as a liquid or as a granule that is watered in, because plants can absorb nutrients only when they are in liquid form. This explains why fertilizer and rich organic soils have so little effect on underwatered plants. The minerals are present, but the plants are unable to absorb

Irrigation and Conservation *(continued)*

Extent of Root System

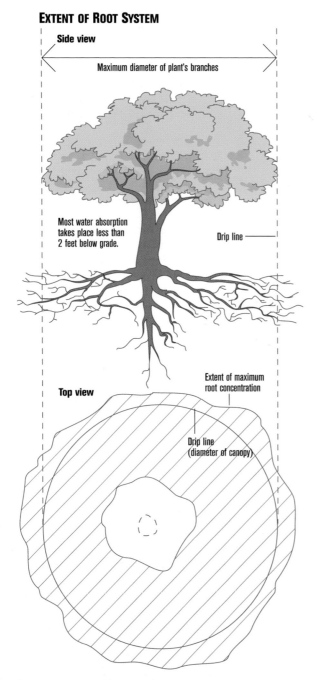

Side view

Maximum diameter of plant's branches

Most water absorption takes place less than 2 feet below grade.

Drip line

Top view

Extent of maximum root concentration

Drip line
(diameter of canopy)

them. In fact fertilizing without supplying adequate water harms plants by causing root hairs to dry out.

■ **Roots and the drip line:** Because roots absorb almost all the water a plant requires (leaves absorb only small amounts), it is helpful to understand how they grow. Some roots, especially those of tall trees and desert shrubs, grow to great depths. The main job of these roots is to anchor the plants or to find water during extreme drought. Most other roots—including those most active in the absorption of water and minerals and in plant respiration— are within 2 feet of the surface of the soil.

Most tree and shrub root systems spread out horizontally a great distance from the stem of the plant. It used to be believed that the longest roots extended as far as the longest branch. An imaginary circle was drawn at this distance, and all watering was to be done within this drip line. It is now known that roots also extend well beyond the drip line. However, as you plot the watering needs of trees and shrubs, drawing a drip line is still a useful exercise, because most roots tend to be concentrated within a few feet on either side of the line.

Water conservation

Home irrigation could appear wasteful, but it is actually less so than conventional watering. The average oscillating sprinkler loses almost as much of its moisture to the atmosphere as goes to water the garden. The droplets it shoots high into the air

◀ **Choose sprinkler heads or adjust them to spray odd-shaped areas of lawn without overspraying onto walks or driveways.**

▶ **Properly installed, a microsprinkler system is efficient and unobtrusive.**

begin to evaporate before reaching the plant. Water evaporates from the foliage before it sinks into the ground, especially in sunny or windy weather. Typically, too, a homeowner sets up a sprinkler and doesn't come back to turn it off until the ground is so saturated that water is running into the street. Water is also wasted over patios and walkways because movable sprinklers are hard to adjust to the actual shapes of individual growing areas.

High-pressure sprinkler irrigation is much more efficient. See page 40. Designed to meet the needs of a specific yard, it sprays only lawns and gardens, not pavement. Irrigation segments are linked in zones to supply water to plants with common needs. The water-hungry lawn can be moistened separately from a mass planting of drought-tolerant shrubs or deep-rooted trees. Slopes are notoriously hard to water. Most water simply runs off, leaving hillside plantings parched. By placing sloped areas on a separate system, it is possible to water them a little at a time, more frequently.

Microirrigation is even more efficient. See page 72. As water penetrates the soil, drop by drop, often under a cover of protective mulch, almost no moisture is lost to direct evaporation. A microirrigation system, or drip system, as it is sometimes called, can be set up to deliver water exactly where it is needed—to the eager roots of vegetable plants, for example—while keeping the spaces between the rows so dry that weeds don't have a chance to sprout. Even individual flower pots on a patio can be watered while the surrounding wooden deck or paving stones remain completely dry. With carefully planned drip irrigation,

A HISTORY OF IRRIGATION

Irrigation has been practiced for thousands of years. The first known traces of irrigation were found in Mesopotamia and date back to about 4000 b.c. These early efforts involved simple canals used to carry water to areas that didn't have enough. As time passed, irrigation techniques became more sophisticated. Using complicated systems of dikes and levees, plus human and animal power, the Mesopotamians carried water many miles from the nearest source and lifted it to great heights, enabling them to create the famous Hanging Gardens of Babylon around 600 b.c. By then, irrigation techniques had appeared in civilizations throughout the world, including Egypt, China, and Europe.

The Romans used pipes to carry water from one place to another; less water evaporates from pipes than from canals. Across the Mediterranean, the Sahara was already dotted with artificial oases supplied by irrigation. Irrigation also appeared simultaneously in the New World: Aztec, Incan, and Mayan cultures all used it. In fact much of the credit for their success can be traced to irrigation, which made it possible to produce the enormous quantities of food needed to support their burgeoning populations.

Irrigation techniques have not always been limited to agricultural uses. Display gardens in Roman atria depended on water brought in from elsewhere, and estate gardens have long used irrigation. The use of sprinkler systems in home landscaping first became popular after World War II, and even drip irrigation, which sounded newfangled only a few years ago, has now become well established. The latest trend—and the thrust of this book—has been the development of user-friendly systems that anyone can install. You are not wandering blindfolded into unknown territory but, rather, are taking advantage of generations of technological advances.

▲ This garden is reminiscent of the Hanging Gardens of Babylon, perhaps the most famous example of irrigation, dating from ancient times.

as much as 80 percent of the water goes to the plants rather than to the atmosphere. With conventional watering, that figure can be as low as 20 percent.

Capturing rainwater

Tens of thousands of gallons of rain run off most roofs, only to soak into the ground beneath downspouts. Capturing this water not only supplements water otherwise taken from your well or municipality, it also solves rainwater runoff problems.

By directing rainwater underground into a gravel-filled area *(below)*, you can put it to good use. A rain barrel *(right)* equipped with a spigot for hooking up a hose (an overflow drain is a wise addition as well) is a simple way to put some of the excess rainwater to use. Some towns sell plastic rain barrels at a subsidized rate to encourage rainwater capture.

In areas where water is particularly precious, some homeowners invest in above- or belowground cisterns to store rainwater for irrigation. Cistern tanks can be made from concrete, galvanized steel, fiberglass, or plastic. Like a rain barrel, a cistern holds excess rainwater until it can be used for home irrigation. Choose a cistern capacity that suits your needs and the amount of rain your area receives. A common range is 1,600 to 2,000 gallons.

An aboveground cistern has the advantage of providing gravity-fed water;

▷ **A new twist on the old wooden rain barrel, this plastic reservoir captures rainwater. If the barrel is high enough above planting areas, a hose can be attached to the spigot for watering.**

▽ **A catch basin holds and slowly distributes rainwater to large planting areas.**

a belowground cistern will require a pump. However, an aboveground unit can be unsightly and must have a suitable footing to keep it stable. Both should be covered for safety, to keep insects from breeding, and to reduce the growth of algae in the water.

Direct rainwater away from the house to a lower spot in the landscape.

Cover the planting bed surface with a layer of mulch.

Use a porous mixture of soil and organic matter to create good drainage in the collection area.

Whether above- or belowground, a cistern should have a 24-inch-diameter access hatch for cleaning. Hatches on underground units should extend at least 8 inches above grade. Provide an overflow line to vent excess water.

Install leaf protection on any gutters and above any downspouts that feed into the cistern. The water will also need to be filtered to avoid clogging any pumps and valves downline, especially if the cistern will be used as a water source for a sprinkler system. Pumps are available with floating filters that draw water from 1 foot below the surface, avoiding surface debris that might otherwise clog the pump.

The system shown below includes a holding tank where debris can settle before the water is drawn off for use. As the water enters the holding tank, an easily accessible nylon mesh bag catches larger debris. A replaceable filter can be added to the outflow pipe to further clarify the water.

Use 4-inch PVC pipe to convey the water to the cistern. Slope horizontal runs ¼ inch per foot and install a clean-out for any run longer than 100 feet. To reduce clogging, use a maximum of 45-degree bends in horizontal runs.

To meld cistern-supplied water with your sprinkler system water supply, consider installing a fill valve in the cistern so there is always enough water to supply your irrigation system while it is running.

▼ While a sizeable investment, a rain-capture system like this can supplement or even replace well water or municipal sources for land-scape irrigation. The system can be adapted to store gray water as well.

Reclaiming water

"Gray" water—water that has been used for bathing or washing clothes—can be diverted and used for irrigating lawns and ornamental plants. In fact, in some arid regions municipalities supply treated reclaimed water to homes through a separate delivery system and require it be used for irrigation.

However, adding your own gray-water storage system is more complex than it might seem. It requires that your home have a dedicated drain system—an expensive proposition. In addition the whole household must understand what can and cannot go into the gray-water system. Small oversights can introduce bacteria into the system, turning the water from gray to septic. Any water containing bodily waste or fluids—even waste water from washing the dog—can create a bacterial hazard.

The ideal gray-water system includes rainwater to dilute the gray water. Stored water should not be left for extended periods of time; systems that are used frequently have less chance for bacterial buildup. An annual dose of chlorine can help forestall bacterial problems, but it is not a substitute for being careful about what goes into the system.

Be sure to consult with your city or county health department before installing a gray-water reclaiming system.

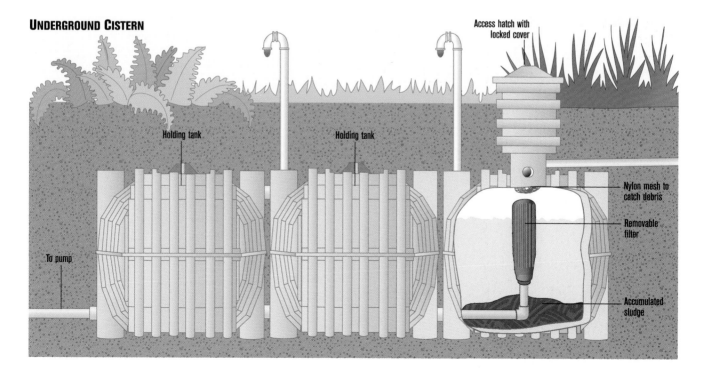

UNDERGROUND CISTERN

Access hatch with locked cover

Holding tank

Holding tank

To pump

Nylon mesh to catch debris

Removable filter

Accumulated sludge

IRRIGATION AND LOCAL CONDITIONS

The homeowner struggling to maintain a green lawn in parched Arizona does not have the same needs as a backyard gardener in the cool and rainy Northwest. Here are guidelines for adapting irrigation to your specific requirements.

Irrigation for all climates

Irrigation systems are not just for hot, dry climates where lack of rain is a constant concern, but for all areas. Plants grow best when they receive adequate amounts of water throughout their growing season; even the short periods of drought that occur in otherwise moist climates can set back growth. Plants in moist climates, in fact, are often more seriously harmed by drought than are those in dry areas because they are not commonly selected for their drought tolerance.

Most yards, regardless of the climate, have sections that receive less natural moisture than others. Areas such as slopes and spots under shallow-rooted trees or beneath roof overhangs often do not retain or receive much water. The plants there may suffer from drought stress. It is a rare yard that could not benefit from one form or another of irrigation.

Watering restrictions

In recent years local watering restrictions have become commonplace. During the summer months it is often no longer possible to water whenever you like; you have to heed the dictates of the municipality in which you live. Some water districts limit the days that you may water; others specify the times of the day, usually late evening when industrial and domestic water use is at its lowest. During an extreme

ANNUAL RAINFALL DISTRIBUTION

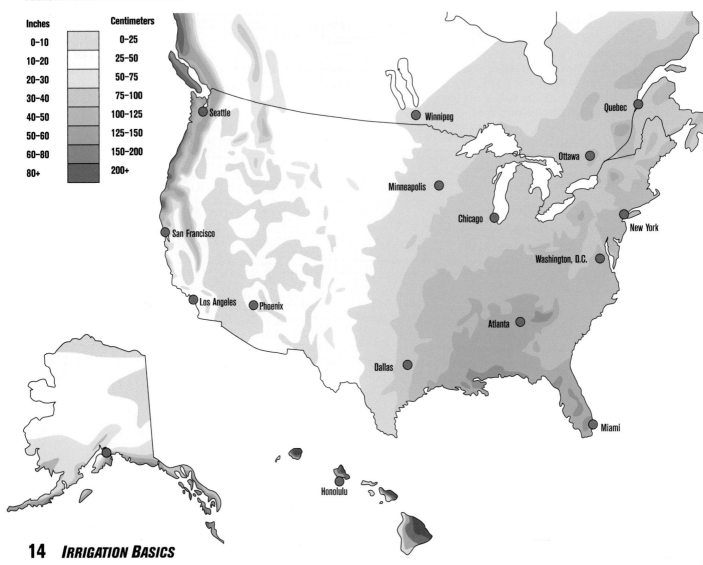

Inches	Centimeters
0–10	0–25
10–20	25–50
20–30	50–75
30–40	75–100
40–50	100–125
50–60	125–150
60–80	150–200
80+	200+

drought, watering may be prohibited for ornamental plants. Even under such restrictions home irrigation allows you to make the maximum use of a limited resource.

When summer water restrictions are in effect, you can easily adjust the timer to turn on the irrigation system at the time specified by municipal regulations. Under severe drought conditions, ornamentals that previously were properly irrigated have a greater chance of survival than do nonirrigated plants.

When watering landscape ornamentals is prohibited, you'll usually still have the option to water food plants. If your vegetable garden is on a separate irrigation circuit, you can keep it going. Plants that have been watered correctly throughout their existence will have healthy, extensive root systems that will allow them to cope better with the stress of drought.

Climate and microclimate

Irrigation requirements vary from region to region and season to season. In North America, irrigation needs are moderate in the Northeast and increase dramatically toward the Southwest. In areas with dusty, dry summer climates, such as

Arizona and much of California, irrigation not only is recommended but often is essential to maintain any semblance of a green landscape.

Under arid conditions, installing lawn and garden irrigation is a matter of course when landscaping a yard or growing vegetables. Total annual rainfall, however, is not the only factor to consider. In the Pacific Northwest, for example, annual precipitation can reach 50 inches or more. The local vegetation is often referred to as rain forest, yet many areas experience severe and prolonged summer droughts. Precipitation is heavy from fall through spring but much lighter in the summer. In other climates, notably in the Midwest and the East, average rainfall is relatively steady from month to month, but droughts can occur, and several dry years in a row will create havoc with even well-established plantings. In such circumstances an irrigation system can be beneficial.

Microclimate refers to very localized conditions—usually resulting from varying exposure to sun or protection from wind. You'll find that within your yard, there are different microclimates—areas that can be warmer or cooler, drier or more humid, than the rest of the landscape. Consider microclimates as you plan a system.

▲ **This lush oasis may appear to be a water waster, but pinpoint irrigation and large shade trees ensure optimum use of limited water.**

■ Obstructions: You will need to watch out for the rain-shadow effect. This occurs in areas that are protected from the prevailing winds by structures or plantings and, therefore, don't receive as much moisture as other parts of the yard. They may need considerably more irrigation than do the areas more exposed to natural rainfall. Gardens under roof overhangs or covered walkways may be so dry they require an irrigation system even in an otherwise wet climate.

■ Temperature: The hotter the air, the faster water evaporates, and the sooner plants will need water again. Because temperatures in North America tend to be higher in southern areas, so are watering needs, even when the amount of rainfall is similar to that of a cooler climate. Likewise, when periods without rain do occur, they tend to cause less damage in northern climates, where cool summers cause less evaporation.

Temperature variations can affect irrigation even within the average home landscape: Sunny lawns and beds are hotter than semishady or shady ones and lose more water to evaporation.

■ Humidity: More water evaporates into dry air than into humid air, and air tends to be drier in the interior of the continent and more humid along the coast and near large bodies of water, such as the Great Lakes. Homeowners in interior regions of the continent will need to irrigate more than gardeners in coastal areas. Besides irrigating

SOIL MOISTURE

Evenly Moist Soil

Waterlogged Soil

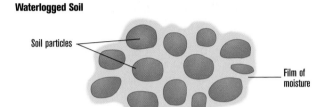

▲ Too much water can be as harmful as too little water. Overwatering forces out air pockets essential to root development.

more frequently, gardeners in dry climates should consider using mulch around their plantings to reduce the evaporation rate.

■ Wind: Strong winds carry off moist air, causing plants to transpire more and lose moisture. Hedges, windbreaks, and plantings of shrubs and trees can reduce the influence of the wind and decrease irrigation needs, even in parts of the country where strong, dry winds are common. If parts of your garden are exposed to drying winds, plan to irrigate them on a separate circuit.

SOIL PARTICLES

Soil is composed of particles of various sizes; each type affects the drainage characteristics of the soil.

Type	Particle Size	Texture When Wet	Texture When Dry	Drainage	Notes
Clay	Very fine-grained	Mucky and slippery; can be kneaded in the hand like bread dough	Becomes compact and hard, like rock; often cracks	Very poor to none	Clay can absorb water and minerals; it is hard to moisten, but if dampened it remains moist for a long time
Silt	Fine but larger-grained than clay	Packs together well but can't be kneaded	Breaks up readily into a flourlike powder	Poor	Silt drains better than clay but not as well as sand
Sand	Large particles	Harsh and gritty to the touch; doesn't hold together	Holds together poorly or not at all; can't be squeezed	Water drains right through; retains little moisture	Individual grains are visible to the naked eye
Gravel	Very large particles	Doesn't hold together	Doesn't hold together	Water drains right through; dries out almost immediately	Individual particles can easily be picked up with the fingers

Types of topsoil

Soil type is an often-overlooked factor when planning home irrigation. However, because it influences how fast water enters and drains from a soil, and how much water the soil holds, it is one of the most important factors.

Natural soils are rarely composed of one type of soil. Most are mixtures containing varying amounts of clay, silt, sand, and humus (an organic material). A mixture containing nearly equal amounts of the different soil types is called loam. Loam falls into various categories, depending on which type of soil predominates. Whether the soil is sand, silt or clay influences how often watering is needed, how long the sprinklers need to run, and how fast the water should flow from the nozzles.

Clay: Clay soils are fertile reservoirs of water and nutrients, but they have tight pores that affect infiltration and drainage. Water puddles on the soil surface and is slow to soak in. Where clay predominates, plan your irrigation system so that it applies water at a very slow rate. Or set it up to cycle off and on in short bursts. Cycling applies water until it starts to puddle, then shuts off to let the water soak in. This pattern should continue until the root zone is moist.

Sandy soil: Sandy soils tend to be dry and infertile. Because minerals are easily washed out of the root zone, plants grown in sandy soil are more likely to suffer nutrient deficiencies and require light but frequent feeding or the use of continuous release plant food. Because sandy soil retains little moisture, there is no use watering abundantly: Most of the water simply drains away. For sandy soil, plan an irrigation system that can apply water quickly and run often enough to support plants' needs.

Silty soil: Because silt is fairly fine-textured, silty soils hold minerals and water well, and most plants thrive in them. Drainage problems may arise in silty loams that contain more clay than sand. Plan your sprinkler system around the soil's dominant characteristics.

Gravel: If the soil is mainly gravel, expect your lawn to have bare patches and your garden poor yields. To improve results, work topsoil and compost into the soil.

▼ **Knowledge of your soil makeup is essential to planning and operating your home irrigation system.**

Subsoil drainage

Having top-quality loam doesn't always guarantee good drainage. Most lots are covered with a relatively thin layer of topsoil of moderate to good quality. Under this is a deep layer of subsoil that is generally low in nutrients and either so sandy that it drains too well or so heavy in clay that it barely supports root growth. In some areas the topsoil is directly on top of

Clay

Sand

Loam

Silt

Gravel

PERFORMING A JAR TEST

Fill a glass jar about one-third full with soil from your yard. Remove all rocks and any plant matter such as stems and roots beforehand. Measure the total depth of the

soil. Add water to the jar, along with a tablespoon of detergent. Cap the jar and shake vigorously to separate individual soil particles. Let the jar sit for 10 minutes,

then shake again. Divide the depth of each layer that settles out by the total depth to learn the percentage of each soil type in your yard and which one predominates.

Within 40 seconds, sandy particles will settle completely and can leave the water looking fairly clear, though dark. Measure the depth of this layer.

After six hours, intermediate size particles—silt—will have settled out. Measure the depth of this layer.

Clay soil particles can take two weeks to settle, leaving a distinct line of clay at the top of the settled material and fairly clear water. Measure the depth of this layer.

IDENTIFYING SOIL TYPE WITH THE FEEL TEST

Begin by picking up some soil from your yard or garden. Rub it back and forth several times in your hands and feel it carefully.

■ A predominantly sandy soil is gritty and doesn't stick together well. Coarse to fine sand has a moderately gritty feel and doesn't hold together when squeezed.

■ A clay soil is slick and smooth, with little or no grittiness. Clay soils are sticky and moldable when wet, and hard and compact when dry.

■ Silt feels smooth and floury when dry, and silky when wet. Organic matter makes a soil feel smoother, as if there were more silt in it.

Next squeeze the soil in your hand. Does it hold together or fall through your fingers? Does it feel sticky?

■ Sandy soil, when squeezed in your hand, feels gritty and doesn't hold together. Moist sandy soil can be pressed into a ball, but it will not hold its shape and will break apart easily.

■ Clay soil when squeezed feels sticky and forms an impression of your fingers. It can be shaped into a long ribbon that holds together well.

■ Silty loam is a good, easy soil to work. A handful of soil can be pressed into a ribbon only about ½ inch long before it breaks apart.

Sand

Clay

Loam

impervious rock or extremely compacted clay called hardpan. Whatever is under the topsoil will affect how frequently you should irrigate.

There is little reason for you to install an irrigation system in a yard that suffers major drainage problems. Why bring in more water if you're already having trouble getting rid of excess moisture? Before you invest in irrigation, identify the problem areas. Improve drainage by installing drainage tiles or pipe, adding high-quality topsoil, solidifying slopes, and otherwise ensuring excess water will drain quickly.

A soil drainage test

To get a better idea of the drainage capacity of the soil in your yard, conduct a soil drainage test. If your yard is uniformly flat and of one soil type, you need test in only one spot. However, if you suspect that you have areas that drain differently due to slope or varying soil types, you may have to do several tests. Choose a day when the soil is relatively dry. Dig a hole about a foot deep and a foot across. Pour a bucket of water into the hole.

■ **Quick drainage:** If the water drains out almost as fast as you can pour it in, your subsoil is probably sandy and drains too well. You will need to irrigate frequently to keep the soil from drying out.

■ **Moderate drainage:** If the hole fills with water, then drains within a few minutes, you have good to fair drainage. Irrigation is especially easy and effective with such soils.

▲ **Building raised beds is an excellent way to overcome poor drainage and other soil problems.**

▶ **A simple drainage test can help you confirm what areas of your property have drainage problems. If a hole filled with water drains in a few minutes, your soil provides good to fair drainage.**

■ **Slow drainage:** If the water is very slow to drain, your soil has poor drainage. Add drainage tiles or pipe before installing an irrigation system, and improve the soil through soil amendments such as compost. If you are not ready for such large-scale modifications, consider raised beds filled with good topsoil for vegetable plots and small flower gardens.

SOIL DRAINAGE TEST

Hole 1' deep, 1' wide

INVESTING IN IRRIGATION

Although irrigation makes landscape maintenance easier, helps you deliver just the right amount of water to each type of plant, and may actually reduce your water bill, irrigation will not pay for itself for a long time if your watering needs are only occasional. It is well worth asking if an irrigation system is right for your property.

Is irrigation necessary?

Just as swimming pools sell like hot cakes during a long, hot summer, irrigation systems are often bought in a rush during a drought. Think back over the last few years. If watering has been a chore almost every summer, installing an irrigation system will be well worthwhile. If most summers in your area are relatively rainy, and you water only a few times in the average year, don't be swayed by one dry summer. Of course even in a moist-summer climate, a few spots, such as under roof overhangs, do require constant attention. If you have such places consider a system for just those areas, rather than an all-encompassing one for the entire yard. A simple soaker hose, easily hidden with mulch and turned on manually, will cost only a few dollars yet take care of an exceptionally dry bed in a climate that otherwise has sufficient rainfall.

Irrigation may not be a necessity if you enjoy hand watering and are generally available during the growing season. Just because your neighbors all have irrigation systems, you don't have to follow suit. Only you know whether the watering you have to carry out is an unbearably heavy chore or a pleasant interlude that keeps you active and in contact with the natural world.

▼ **Irrigating a difficult corner, such as a flower bed under eaves, can be as simple as laying a length of porous soaker hose.**

The right time

Consider irrigation only when a future landscape is mapped out on paper and the major infrastructures, such as retaining walls, are in place. Irrigation pipes, though solid, will not stand up to bulldozers, and sprinkler heads can be torn off during even minor landscaping projects.

The ideal time for installing irrigation, if your budget allows it, is toward the end of your landscape project, when all the hardscaping is in place, topsoil has been brought in and leveled, trees and shrubs have been planted, and all that is left to do is to put in the perennials, turf, and mulches. Irrigation piping will be easy to install in the loose soil and will be quickly hidden from sight by the final plantings.

Future upgrades

Although it is always ideal to install a system that suits your yard perfectly, irrigation systems can be improved as needs change or when you decide to add to your landscaping. Systems can be fully manual, fully automated, or a combination of the two. Timers can be expanded. Spray nozzles can be changed if you decide to substitute one type of plant for another. Traditional sprinkler zones can be converted to drip or microirrigation if you decide to add a flower bed or a vegetable patch. Even adding new zones is straightforward, as long as they are allowed for in your initial plan.

LANDSCAPING FOR MINIMAL IRRIGATION

Consider planning your landscape to reduce the need for irrigation. Using drought-tolerant plants and water-conserving techniques is practical in just about every climate. However, even drought-tolerant plants require some watering, especially during the first year or two of growth. And, of course, you might want to reserve the luxury of a few lush, green oases maintained by irrigation.

Xeriscaping

Xeriscaping is a relatively new concept in landscape design. Created in 1981 in Denver, Colorado as a response to frequent droughts and water shortages, Xeriscaping refers to landscape design that requires minimal irrigation to flourish. The name is derived from the Greek word *xeros* (dry). Xeriscaped yards need not be dry, barren landscapes, however, nor are they maintenance-free. The practice encourages the use of native or well-adapted plants. A Xeriscape can be as simple or complex as the gardener or designer wishes.

▼ **Xeriscaping typically mandates keeping thirsty plants close to the house, and minimizing trenching and extensive plumbing.**

Based on sound horticulture, Xeriscaping works in any environment, with a variety of landscape designs. Use it successfully with Japanese, Southwestern, cottage, and other formal and natural-looking gardens. Xeriscaping uses drought-tolerant plants (native, if possible) and water-saving strategies to create lawns and gardens that do not consume excessive amounts of irrigation water. Plants well adapted to Xeriscaping vary from region to region. Check with your local county extension service for a list of plants that are suited to your area.

Xeriscapes are divided into zones with different water requirements. The oasis zone is an area located closest to the house where most human activity occurs. Plants in this zone have the highest water needs and may also require more maintenance. This is usually the most colorful area of the landscape.

Beyond the oasis zone is a transition zone of moderate water use. This zone contains plants that require infrequent irrigation and, usually, less maintenance.

▶ Although ideal for arid regions, Xeriscaping can be used anywhere to create a hardy, water-smart yard. Here a palo verde tree contributes shade, agaves and cactus provide texture, and Mexican evening primrose adds color.

The outermost zone is a low-water-use zone, which requires no supplemental water or only infrequent irrigation during prolonged dry periods.

Use plants well adapted to your area, combined with mulches that suppress weeds and conserve water, plus drip irrigation to design a Xeriscape that offers color and fragrance with only monthly or seasonal maintenance.

By applying the basic principles of Xeriscaping to your landscape, you can conserve valuable water resources and create a yard that is both beautiful and easy to maintain.

■ **Group plants:** For greatest irrigation efficiency, design your yard so that plants with similar water needs are grouped in the same area. This makes maintenance easier and irrigation more efficient.

■ **Irrigate seasonally:** Adjust your watering schedule to reflect seasonal changes in the water needs of your plants. Irrigation requirements change greatly through the course of the year. Spring may bring sufficient rainfall, whereas summer may require heavier irrigation.

■ **Practice good irrigation design:** Make sure that irrigated areas are covered uniformly, with no over- or underwatered spots. Good design uses irrigation technology most appropriate to the plants being watered.

■ **Limit turf:** Grow lawn only where you need it, for example, in recreational and play areas. Avoid using lawn on steep slopes, in shady areas, in narrow spaces, or in other areas that are difficult to water and mow. Where appropriate, plant groundcovers instead of lawn.

■ **Create plant islands:** Arrange water-hungry, high-maintenance plants in accent groupings around the yard rather than spread out over large, difficult-to-water areas.

■ **Choose plants carefully:** Choose plants suited to your environment, such as native plants or those from a similar climate.

■ **Create a patio:** Use hardscape design elements that don't need water, such as patios and decks, to enhance your outdoor environment. Choose appropriate materials to complement your plantings as well.

Hydrozoning

Traditionally irrigation systems have been divided into areas called circuits (also referred to as zones). Circuits are sections of an irrigation system that have a number of sprinkler devices sharing the same water lines and a common irrigation valve, with each of the circuits controlled independently by the irrigation timer. Circuits were first used to maintain proper water pressure in the water pipes feeding the irrigation system, and as a means of configuring a portion of a watering system for particular types of crops.

Often the number of sprinkler heads needed to water an area, and the resulting pressure and flow needed by the system to run them, exceeds the pressure and flow that are available from the water source. Each independent circuit can be sized so it won't overtax the irrigation water system. As a result the optimum water pressure and flow are always maintained.

Hydrozoning extends the zone concept. As the cost of irrigation components has fallen and timers have become more sophisticated, it has become possible to plan and install circuits to allow for more specific watering of your plants. For instance, in a traditional layout there might be three or four circuits to water the front and back lawns and a couple of planting beds. In a hydrozoned landscape, you might find as many as ten circuits, each one targeted to a specific plant type. These smaller zones can be set precisely to distribute only the amount of water the plant groupings require.

From a planning perspective, in order for hydrozoning to work correctly and be practical to install, landscapes need to be arranged in such a way that plants with compatible water needs are located on the same circuits. This requires a different approach to landscape planning, and it often yields surprisingly good results.

Hydrozoning was first used in arid climates, where plants were divided into groupings of high, moderate, and low water use, defined as follows.

■ **High water use:** These are the thirstiest plants, such as lawns, blooming annuals, and vegetables.

■ **Moderate water use:** Plants in this category need more water than nature provides. Usually they need irrigation only while getting established and during long dry spells.

■ **Low water use:** These plants survive with only the water available locally. They are good for planting on slopes that are difficult to irrigate.

▼ **Hydrozoning delivers the right amount of water to plants, preserving the water supply while helping the plants flourish.**

GETTING STARTED

HOW TO MEASURE, EVALUATE, AND PLAN

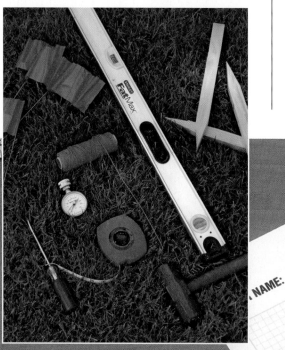

efore shopping for your irrigation system, you have a good deal of homework to do. Take a serious look at your yard, its needs, and your budget. Confirm the water capacity of your home and any municipal water restrictions. Draw up a detailed plan of the lot showing any factors that will affect the irrigation system. Expect to do several versions; the plan will help you spot problem areas and work out necessary solutions. If you have any doubts or areas of confusion, consult a professional or take advantage of the planning services provided by major irrigation-component manufacturers. See page 26. It's far better to uncover a mistake at the planning stage when your project exists only on paper than to discover a major flaw after the system is installed.

Remember, too, that it is premature to install an irrigation system until you know all the details of the landscaping project. Whether you are moving into a new home or planning to change your yard, wait until the landscape plan is completed on paper before considering irrigation. Once this is done, you have a basic decision to make: Do you want a sprinkler system or a microirrigation system? Each has its own advantages, so before proceeding you'll need to consider all the factors discussed in this chapter.

▼ **A detailed plan takes time to execute but is an essential step in developing an irrigation scheme that suits the needs of your landscape.**

TWO IMPORTANT QUESTIONS

▶ **A pipe puller can install poly or PVC pipe (shown here) quickly, with little mess. It is best adapted to large, flat lawn areas.**

Before you begin to draw up plans for an irrigation system, you'll first have to resolve two questions: Can I do the work myself, or should I hire a professional? Should I use sprinkler irrigation or microirrigation? This section will help you make up your mind.

Do it yourself or hire a professional?

Do-it-yourself irrigation is becoming more and more feasible. In some parts of the country, homeowners install nearly 75 percent of all irrigation systems. Installing an irrigation system is well within the reach of a capable homeowner who plans thoroughly and works carefully. But digging trenches, installing piping, making connections, and fine-tuning constitutes a lengthy process. Allow several weekends to get the entire system up and running.

All this work does require physical effort, but it isn't backbreaking so long as you work carefully. You need little in the way of specialized equipment, and what you do need you can often rent. Doing the job yourself usually costs about one-half to two-thirds as much as having the system professionally installed. However, a poorly installed system could require extensive revisions, diminishing any savings you derived from doing the job yourself. At certain stages in the process, you may be able to hire professional help without incurring major expense.

■ **Learn all you can:** Clinics and workshops provide a good introduction to irrigation. Many irrigation specialists offer them regularly, often free of charge. These clinics give you a chance to see how irrigation systems are planned and installed and to ask a few basic questions. Contact a dealer or a local horticultural society to find out about clinics and workshops in your area.

If you have access to the Internet, you can take advantage of the planning and training information offered by manufacturers such as Orbit, Rain Bird, and Toro. Their sites include interactive manuals and product information, as well as downloadable installation guides and catalogs. See box, at left.

■ **Planning aids:** To avoid the most costly errors, you may want to consult with a professional irrigator during the planning stage. Exact spray patterns are hard to plot, and professionals are aware of specialized sprinklers and emitters for specific needs.

PLANNING SERVICES

Although a local irrigation specialist may have the best knowledge of irrigation requirements for your specific climate and the municipal regulations that apply to installing a system, the free planning assistance provided by major sprinkler manufacturers is well worth considering.

Some manufacturers provide questionnaires and mapping aids that you can fax or mail in for planning assistance. Others provide you with planning software you can download and use on your home computer. However, to use these aids you will still have to measure and map out your lot and procure specific information about your water system. That typically includes a detailed landscape plan, water meter location, and pressure and flow information as well as data about special situations like slopes.

What you'll get in return is a detailed plan, installation instructions, and a complete shopping list—using the manufacturer's components, of course.

In addition, irrigation systems are being constantly improved and updated. Without consulting an expert, you may have difficulty finding the most appropriate materials for your situation. Professional help is especially useful if your property has special needs or unusual conditions, such as extreme slopes or poor drainage.

Consult with people who specialize in irrigation systems. Salespeople at home centers or hardware stores may know less than they think they know. Consulting need not be expensive. Many dealers will produce a plan without charge if you buy the parts from them. Others charge a small fee, but you may find that the advice is worth the expense. Follow the instructions in this chapter to gather the proper information and to draw an accurate plot of your lot. The dealer will indicate the installations you need and supply a complete list of parts.

Trenching for pipes: You might also consider professional help when installing the piping. Digging shallow trenches is well within the capacity of most homeowners, but it is time-consuming and messy. A professional using trench-digging equipment can do the job more easily and quickly, often at an affordable price.

Trenching equipment such as trenchers and pipe-pullers (also called vibratory plows) are available from rental stores.

Trenchers, as their name suggests, dig narrow trenches in the soil for both rigid PVC and flexible polyethylene (poly) piping. If you are using flexible polyethylene pipe and your soil is easily workable and not too rocky, a pipe-puller is suited to the job. This apparatus cuts a narrow slit in the lawn and then pulls the pipe through the ground, leaving the pipe ends exposed so you can add connections. The damage to the lawn is so minor that it heals in a few days.

Trenchers and pipe-pullers are most useful on large, open, flat areas. They are of little advantage on slopes; in small yards with lots of corners to turn; or in large yards with raised beds, terracing, trees, or other obstacles. These machines, especially tractor-driven ones, need a considerable amount of space in which to maneuver; running them on anything other than large, flat areas or minor slopes can be dangerous.

Experience with the equipment helps. It takes skill to dig at the correct depth and to maintain the depth uniformly along the entire length of a trench.

Problem areas: In a few situations it is best to leave the installation work entirely to professionals. If you have severe erosion

▼ A trenching machine digs narrow trenches quickly. Such a machine can be rented from a rental agency or a home center.

problems, very rocky soils, steep slopes, and delicate plantings that need protection, you may want to hire a professional installer. One of the advantages of consulting a professional at the planning stage is learning whether you have any problem areas such as these.

■ **Plumbing:** You may not have the option of installing the pipe leading to your irrigation system yourself. Many cities require that a licensed plumber install the line from the city main to the backflow preventer (the beginning of the irrigation system). If this is the case, you can still save money by preparing the work site beforehand. Determine the proper placement of the piping and backflow preventer, prepare any trenches or holes, and have all necessary parts on hand before the plumber gets there, so the job is strictly limited to installing the pipes. If your municipality has no such restrictions, you can install the pipe and backflow preventer yourself. It is relatively easy to cut pipe and install a tee. See page 64.

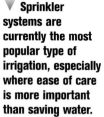

▼ **Sprinkler systems are currently the most popular type of irrigation, especially where ease of care is more important than saving water.**

Sprinkler or microirrigation?

Probably no irrigation question is more confusing to the average homeowner than whether to install a high-pressure sprinkler system or a low-pressure microirrigation system. It is hard to determine which is the best overall, and the line between the two systems is quickly disappearing. You'll have to consider the advantages and disadvantages of each and decide which is best in your case.

■ **Sprinkler systems:** High-pressure, or sprinkler irrigation is by far the most common system in North America. When most people think of home irrigation, they think of a high-pressure sprinkler system. These systems use water piped under high pressure to spray the landscape.

Sprinkler systems are almost entirely underground. The sprinkler heads are the only visible components of a well-designed sprinkler system, and even these are generally unobtrusive or disappear underground when not in use. Because sprinkler systems require considerable

◀ Microirrigation can be concealed by burying service lines and covering emitters with mulch.

trenching, they are usually more expensive than microirrigation systems. This isn't to say that microirrigation systems are simpler to install. The time required to assemble the large number of parts of a microirrigation system can be considerable. On the other hand, sprinkler systems normally require less upkeep than do microirrigation systems. Usually all they need are minor adjustments and annual draining. As an investment, sprinkler systems may well be the best choice. Many prospective home buyers are leery of microirrigation, while believing that sprinkler irrigation systems make landscape maintenance a snap.

Sprinkler systems use more water than microirrigation systems but less than conventional watering. Sprinkler systems are most appropriate where ease of care and landscape appearance are more important than water conservation. However, a properly installed sprinkler system is much

▶ An emitter releases water, drop by drop, directly to the base of the plant instead of splashing onto the leaves, where it could foster disease and burn the plant.

▶ **Microirrigation systems are ideal for hanging baskets that need frequent watering.**

less wasteful than one that is incorrectly installed. An overpressurized sprinkler system will produce a foglike spray, with a large percentage of the water blowing away. A correctly installed sprinkler system has just enough pressure to place water just where it is needed and will use water more efficiently.

Many homeowners find sprinkler systems most advantageous on large surfaces and lawns and less so in beds that are frequently dug up or changed, such as vegetable gardens. Rototillers can easily damage a sprinkler head or supply line. It is also difficult to adapt inground sprinkler systems to movable aboveground containers, such as hanging baskets and patio planters.

■ **Microirrigation systems:** Microirrigation systems use small amounts of water at a time. Often the spraying is not readily apparent. In many cases it is barely visible, even when the system is in full operation. Because water is applied at soil level, much less is lost to evaporation, making microirrigation an obvious choice in dry climates where water restrictions are severe. A well-planned microirrigation system leaves the soil surface relatively dry but keeps the root zone constantly moist.

Until fairly recently the most common form of microirrigation was drip irrigation. Now the most commonly used form is a combination of drip and spray applications, which are installed as a surface system. The components of a microirrigation system are often partly hidden by decorative mulches. Because these tubes and emitters are run here and there through the garden, they are more visible than a sprinkler system. However, they have a number of advantages.

Ease of installation: Because digging is not necessary, drip irrigation is easy and inexpensive to install. Some hardware stores and garden centers carry inexpensive drip-irrigation kits that can be installed in a day. All parts of a drip system are easy to reach and the system is highly adaptable. Installing a new emitter may take seconds, whereas adding a new sprinkler head to a sprinkler system is a major undertaking. You can also pull up a drip-irrigation system in minutes if you need to till a bed or take in the system for the winter.

Durability: In the past, breakdown was one of the major flaws of drip-irrigation systems. Emitters were far more likely to clog than were sprinklers, and changing emitters often became a regular and tedious chore. Today well-installed microirrigation

TO DRIP OR TO SPRAY?

Which system—sprinkler or microirrigation—should you choose? Very possibly both, depending on your specific needs. This chart gives an idea of which system is more appropriate in which situations. If in doubt, consult an irrigation professional.

	Sprinkler	Microirrigation
Requires trenching	Yes	Sometimes
Water-saving capacity	Good	Excellent
Essentially invisible	Yes	Sometimes
Expensive to install	Yes	Sometimes
Limited maintenance requirements	Yes	Sometimes
Increases resale value of home	Yes	Sometimes
Additions easily made	Rarely	Often
Good for temporary use	No	Yes
Prevents weed germination	No	Under certain conditions
Helps prevent disease spread	Limited effect	Yes
Supplementary hand watering may be required	Rarely	Sometimes
Can be used on:		
Lawns	Yes	Sometimes
Flower beds	Yes	Yes
Shrubs and trees	Yes	Yes
Vegetable gardens	Sometimes	Yes
Groundcovers	Yes	Yes
Container plants	Sometimes	Yes
Slopes	Sometimes	Yes

systems are not as fragile as some people think. However, because of their more exposed parts, microirrigation systems are not quite as sturdy as sprinkler systems and need a little more care.

Microirrigation service lines can and probably should be buried. Much of the paraphernalia can be hidden under mulch and behind or under plantings. Simple microirrigation systems, such as porous hose, can be inexpensive temporary fixes until you can afford or have time to install a more permanent solution.

Disease prevention: Many plant diseases develop only when leaves are moist. With conventional watering and sprinkler irrigation, diseases are carried to susceptible leaves by drops of water bouncing from the soil. Bubbler heads, which water the ground more than they do the leaves, are often used in sprinkler irrigation when disease is a concern. Even with this precaution, sprinklers are more likely to spread disease than are microirrigation systems that do not moisten the leaves.

Weed control: In climates with little or no summer rainfall, microirrigation can help prevent the spread of weeds. Since the surface of the soil remains dry, weed seeds can't germinate. You can keep surfaces such

WHERE TO USE MICROIRRIGATION

Generally microirrigation is most useful for small yards, vegetable beds, container gardens, and flower beds. You can even use it to water hanging baskets. It is also ideal for watering difficult spots, such as slopes, where much of the water from sprinkler irrigation would otherwise simply run off. Until recently microirrigation has not been considered adaptable to watering lawns, but new subsurface microirrigation systems designed specifically for that use are available.

as the spaces between the rows in your vegetable garden or gravel walks and driveways almost entirely free of vegetation by not irrigating there at all. This is more difficult to accomplish with sprinkler irrigation, where wind-blown spray is much more likely to reach all parts of the yard. The disadvantage of this dry-surface effect is that desirable seed-grown plants won't grow. In a microirrigated vegetable garden, for example, you'll have to hand-water newly sown beds of carrots, lettuce, and corn until the roots of the young plants have reached into the moist soil below.

▼ **Microirrigation systems put the water exactly where it is needed, reducing loss through evaporation.**

A Closer Look at Your Property

Each irrigation case is unique because each depends on a wide range of factors. In this section you'll learn how to determine a vital element in planning your system—the water capacity of your home—as well as how to create a plan of your property.

Measuring water capacity

The first step in installing any irrigation system—particularly a sprinkler-type system—is determining the water capacity of your home. This is not hard to do. The four steps listed below and the charts on the following pages will help you.

1. Check water pressure: The water pressure of a system varies according to how many water-using components are operating, the time of day (pressure is greater from late evening through early morning), and the weather conditions (lower pressure occurs during periods of drought). In most cases you'll need only an average reading of the *static* water pressure, the water pressure available when no water is running inside or outside your house. Your goal is to determine the lowest static water pressure the irrigation system is likely to encounter. That way, as you plan the system, you will know that enough water pressure will reach each sprinkler so it can function correctly.

You may have reason to think the pressure that your irrigation system will receive when it is in operation, the working pressure, will be a good deal lower than the static pressure. For instance you may run the sprinklers while your family is using several water sources in the house. If that is the case, see the box on the facing page.

One way of obtaining static water pressure is to contact the local water company or municipality. This is usually not the best method because the reading they give you is only a sector average. If your home is at a lower or higher elevation, the number may not be accurate. Checking the static water pressure yourself is best.

However, if you live in a new housing development, a reading of the water pressure in your home using a pressure

▲ **A combination flow and pressure gauge is the quickest way to evaluate your home water system.**

Some Questions to Ask

During the course of planning an irrigation system, you will likely need to ask local utility companies or municipal authorities several questions. (If your home was professionally inspected when purchased, some of this information may be in the inspector's report.) Start with these:

■ Where is my water meter located?
■ What is the static water pressure for my sector? Is it expected to drop in the future; if so, to what level?
■ What is the size of my water meter?
■ What is the diameter of my service line?
■ Do I need a permit to install a lawn-and-garden irrigation system?

■ What local codes affect the installation of an underground irrigation system? (Codes can specify the type of pipe and other materials, the type and location of backflow prevention, and the method of tying in to the water main. Also ask whether a licensed plumber is needed for certain installations.)
■ Are there any underground utilities I should be aware of when digging? (Sometimes these are surprisingly close to the surface. Contact gas, phone, electric, water, and cable companies for this information.)
■ Do regulations govern private irrigation on municipal property, such as the planting strip between the sidewalk and the street?

A SIMPLE FLOW TEST

If your service line (the length of pipe between the street and the house) is longer than 75 feet, or if it might be seriously corroded, the flow could be limited—which would result in considerable loss of pressure. The values given in the water-capacity tables (see page 35) assume a static water pressure that is the same as the working pressure of the system. But if the pressure that is actually available when the water is running is severely reduced, the reading you took will not accurately reflect the flow. A quick flow test roughly shows the actual number of gallons per minute of working or operating pressure. Fill a bucket of a known size from an outside faucet. Turn on the water full force, and count the number of seconds it takes to fill the bucket to the brim. To calculate the number of gallons per minute (gpm), simply divide the bucket size in gallons by the number of seconds it took to fill, then multiply this total by 60 seconds. The result is the number of gallons per minute available at the faucet. Here is the formula.

$$\frac{\text{Bucket size (gal.)}}{\text{Seconds to fill}} \times \frac{\text{60 seconds}}{\text{1 minute}} = \text{gpm}$$

For example if a 2-gallon bucket fills with water in 10 seconds, the available flow is 12 gallons per minute.

gauge may actually be less useful than the water company's estimate, because water pressure will drop as additional households are added to the system. Instead ask the water company for its estimate of the future static pressure in your sector.

To check the pressure yourself, attach a water pressure gauge (sometimes combined with flow gauge as shown on the facing page) to an outside faucet. An irrigation-products supplier may lend you one, or you can borrow or rent one from a hardware store. Turn off all water-using equipment (clothes washer, dishwasher, indoor and outdoor faucets, and so on), and ask family members not to turn on water or flush the toilet. Screw the gauge onto an outside faucet. Turn on the faucet completely. Note the results in pounds per square inch (psi).

If possible take the readings in summer when the municipal water level is low. Take note of the pressure levels at different times of the day, then use the lowest one in your calculations because you want the irrigation system to be efficient even when water pressure is low. Well owners should see page 35.

Write the lowest static water pressure reading on your planning sheet or installation guide. For proper system operation, water pressure should not exceed 80 psi. If yours exceeds this amount, install a pressure regulator.

◀ Water meter size is usually stamped on the surface of the meter. The meter can be found outdoors in an underground box or, in colder climates, in a basement or utility room.

The service-line measurement should be taken immediately before the water meter. If you don't have a water meter, measure the pipe running from the street into the house. To determine the circumference of the line, wrap a piece of string around the pipe, then measure the length of the string. The diameter of the interior of the pipe is less than its outside circumference and depends on the thickness of the material from which the pipe is made. Copper pipe, for example, is thinner than galvanized steel or schedule 40 PVC pipe. It is easy to tell the pipes apart. Copper pipe is metallic and reddish bronze; galvanized pipe is a grayish metal; PVC pipe is plastic.

To determine the inner size of the service line, use the Service-Line Dimension Chart *below*. Jot down this measurement next to the static water pressure and the water-meter size.

4. Calculate water capacity: If you are having your system professionally designed, take the measurements (static water pressure, flow, meter size, and service-line size) to the irrigation specialist. If you are designing the system yourself, consult the water-capacity tables on the facing page. Use Table 1 if you have a water meter; Table 2 if you do not.

To use the tables, find your water-meter and service-line sizes in the left columns, then find the static water pressure along the top. The point where the two lines converge gives you the approximate water capacity. For example, if the water meter measures 1 inch, your service line is ¾ inch

2. Check water-meter size: First locate the water meter. If you live in a cold climate, it is probably in the basement. In a warm climate it may be near the street or just outside the house. If you don't know where it is, look it up on the property layout plan you received when you bought the house, or call the local water company.

Water meters usually come in three sizes: ⅝ inch, ¾ inch, or 1 inch. Your meter's measurement should be stamped on the meter. If not, contact the water company. Write down the water-meter size next to the static water pressure. If your system does not use water meters or if you use a well or pressure tank, you won't need to note this factor.

3. Find service-line dimensions: The service line is the main water pipeline running from the street to your home. You need its inner dimensions in order to determine water capacity. The water company or municipality might have this information, especially if your home is new. If not it is easy to check the measurement yourself.

▲ **To find the inner dimension of the service line, wrap a piece of string around the pipe. Measure the string and use the chart below to convert the measurement to the pipe size.**

SERVICE-LINE DIMENSION CHART

Example: If your service line is galvanized steel pipe and it takes 4 inches of string to encircle it, the size of your line is 1 inch.

Length of string	2¾"	3¼"	3½"	4"	4⅜"	5"
Size of copper service line	¾"		1"		1¼"	
Size of galvanized service line			¾"	1"		1¼"
Size of PVC (schedule 40) service line			¾"	1"		1¼"

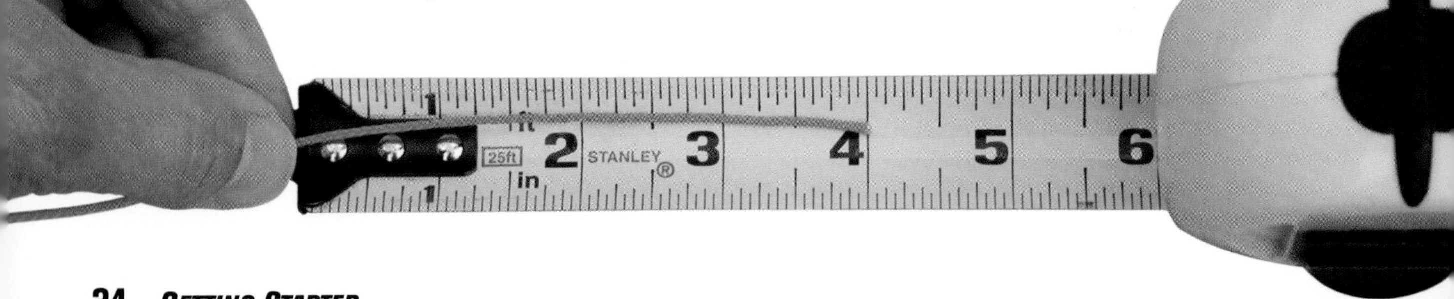

in diameter, and the static water pressure is 55 psi, Table 1 shows you will have a maximum flow of 13.0 gpm for each zone.

Note that the tables are based on a 75-foot copper service line. If your line is PVC, add 2 gpm. If the line is galvanized, subtract 5 gpm. If the service line is significantly longer than 75 feet, contact an irrigation supplier to determine a more specific calculation. Also see how to conduct a simple flow test on page 33.

The water capacity you have determined indicates the maximum amount of water you can count on being able to use at any one time. You'll need this figure when determining how many sprinklers or emitters you can include in one zone.

Wells and pressure tanks

If your water is supplied by a pump or pressure tank, you will need another means of determining water capacity. Check the owner's manual to find the working pressure (in psi) and flow rate (in gpm) of the pump. Alternatively locate the name and number of the pump and contact your well or pump dealer.

ELEVATION CONSIDERATIONS

The water-capacity calculations in Tables 1 and 2 *below* are for relatively flat land. For each foot rise in elevation, there is a corresponding loss of 0.433 psi of pressure. Likewise, for each foot drop, there is a 0.433 psi gain in pressure. Any major differences in elevation in your yard will affect the working pressure.

To take this into account, add or subtract the appropriate factor and recalculate the water capacity in gallons per minute for that sector only. For example, if your static water pressure measured at the house is 55 psi, and one sector of the backyard is 10 feet higher than the house, subtract 5 psi (10 feet x 0.433, rounded off), which gives you a water pressure of 50 psi. Now use the charts again to recalculate the water capacity for that sector.

WATER CAPACITY IN GALLONS PER MINUTE (GPM)

TABLE 1: FOR SYSTEMS WITH A WATER METER (75-FOOT COPPER SERVICE LINE, OR LESS)

Size of water meter	Size of service line	Static water pressure (psi)										
		30	35	40	45	50	55	60	65	70	75	80
⅝"	½"	2.0	3.5	5.0	6.0	6.5	7.0	7.5	8.0	9.0		
⅝"	¾"	3.5	5.0	7.0	8.5	9.5	10.0	11.0	11.5	13.0		
¾"	¾"	6.0	7.5	9.0	10.0	12.0	13.0	14.0	15.0	16.0	17.5	18.5
¾"	1"	7.5	10.0	11.5	13.5	15.0	16.0	17.5	18.5	20.0	21.0	22.0
¾"	1¼"	10.0	12.0	13.0	15.0	17.0	18.0	19.0	21.0	23.0	24.5	26.0
1"	¾"	6.0	7.5	9.0	10.0	12.0	13.0	14.0	15.0	16.0	17.5	18.5
1"	1"	10.0	12.0	13.5	17.0	19.5	22.0	23.5	25.0	26.0	28.0	29.0
1"	1¼"	12.0	15.5	17.5	21.0	23.5	26.0	28.5	30.5	32.5	34.0	35.0

TABLE 2: FOR SYSTEMS WITHOUT A WATER METER (75-FOOT COPPER SERVICE LINE, OR LESS)

Size of service line	Static water pressure (psi)										
	30	35	40	45	50	55	60	65	70	75	80
½"	2.0	3.5	5.0	6.0	6.5	7.0	7.5	8.0	9.0		
¾"	6.0	7.5	9.0	10.0	12.0	13.0	14.0	15.0	16.0	17.5	18.5
1"	10.0	12.0	13.5	17.0	19.5	22.0	23.5	25.0	26.0	28.0	29.0
1¼"	12.0	15.5	17.5	21.0	23.5	26.0	28.5	30.5	32.5	34.0	35.0

DRAWING A PLAN

Whether you intend to draw up the irrigation plan yourself or have a professional do it, you'll need a plot plan of your property. This plan must be as accurate as you can make it; overestimating the needs of your property can be expensive, and underestimating them will result in an irrigation system that does not cover the entire area. To draw your plan you will need both plain paper and graph paper, a pencil and an eraser, a 50- or 100-foot tape measure, a spike, a stake or screwdriver, a ruler, and a compass.

Outline building and property lines

Start by locating, if possible, an existing property layout plan. You probably received one with your deed. If not, you can obtain a copy from the local building department or tax assessor's office. Remember, this plan may or may not include the area between your property line and the street, but if you want to irrigate that area, you'll need to take it into account. If your yard was professionally landscaped, you should have a plan of this as well.

Do not draw directly on any existing plan, but transfer its details to grid paper. Do not assume these existing plans are accurate, since structures or plantings may not have been placed exactly as planned,

and any changes made over the years are probably not shown. Nevertheless, these plans are an excellent basis from which to begin drawing a plot plan.

Make a photocopy of the layout plan that most closely represents the current status of the yard, then recheck the measurements. If no layout plan is available, draw a freehand sketch of the property on plain white paper and pencil in measurements as you go along.

Start measuring with the house, noting all its outside dimensions. Then measure in both directions from the corners of the house to the property lines. A helper can hold one end of the tape measure while you hold the other. If you're doing it on your own, drive a stake or screwdriver through the loop at the end of the measuring tape and into the ground to hold the tape in place.

Once you are sure of the measurements, transfer them to graph paper. An 11- by 17-inch sheet will provide plenty of space to work with, or tape together two sheets of 8½- by 11-inch paper. Most irrigation-system manufacturers provide a piece of graph paper in their installation guidebooks or with their parts list.

Using a convenient scale (1 small square to 1 foot, for example) and a pencil, trace the house onto the plan, then add the property lines. Don't be surprised if the property lines are not perfectly rectangular, even if they appear to be so to the naked eye: Few lots have perfect 90-degree angles at each corner. Don't hesitate to redraw the plan if you make any major errors. It is vital to have an accurate final version.

Once you have plotted the lot and house to your satisfaction, trace the property lines and house with a permanent marker so the details won't be accidentally erased as you work.

Now draw in the permanent features, such as patios, driveways, garages, walks, toolsheds, retaining walls, paving slabs, fences, flagpoles, and pools, taking careful measurements of each. Use the corners of the house as reference points to make sure you've correctly located the features on the plan. Also indicate basement windows or other low windows. You won't want them constantly soaked by sprinklers.

You don't have to mark all measurements on the plan. They will be clearly indicated by the fact you've drawn to scale. If the plan is cluttered, erase less important measurements, leaving those you'll look at regularly when planning, such as the

DRAWING A PROPERTY SKETCH

Make a rough sketch of your property on a plain sheet of paper. Measure the areas to be irrigated. An assistant and a 50- or 100-foot tape measure will make the job go faster. Exact dimensions are not necessary—it's OK to round off to the nearest foot.

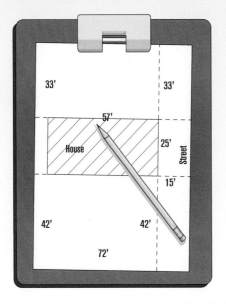

33'   33'

57'

House   25'   Street

15'

42'   42'

72'

length and width of driveways, walks, or flower beds.

Include plants and other elements

Your plot should also include all permanent plantings, including lawns, trees, shrubs, hedges, flower beds, groundcovers, and vegetable beds. Be specific. If you know the names of trees and shrubs, write them down, using a legend if possible to reduce clutter. Take special note of any trees with low-hanging branches that could block spray patterns, and design your system to take their rain shadows into account.

Try to draw the landscape as it will be in the future. In the case of trees, for example, don't indicate only current height and spread but approximate size at maturity. As trees grow, they not only will need more water but also are likely to block sprinklers from reaching parts of the yard. By planning for growth, you can put in sprinklers or emitters that will function for years to come. A good gardening reference book should provide the eventual height and diameter of trees and shrubs. If any

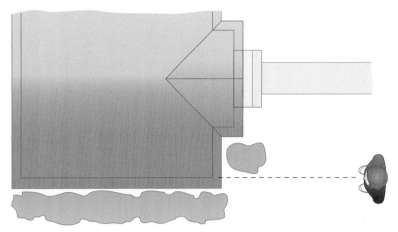

elements of the landscape are planned but not yet installed, be sure to include them in the drawing.

Other elements you should incorporate are the water-supply line, water meter location, and any outdoor faucets. If you use a pump and a well, show them. This information will help you decide where to connect the irrigation system to the supply line. Use a compass to determine which direction is north, and indicate this as well.

▲ **Property lines and all other elements in your yard can be accurately located by using your house as the base from which you take all measurements.**

INITIAL PLOTTING

Scale: 1 square = 1'0"

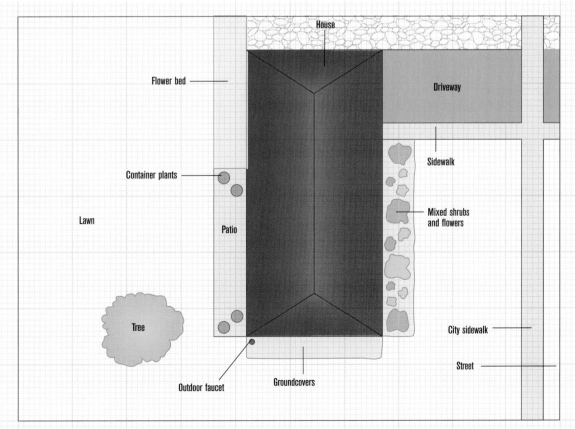

House
Flower bed
Driveway
Sidewalk
Container plants
Mixed shrubs and flowers
Lawn
Patio
Tree
City sidewalk
Street
Outdoor faucet
Groundcovers

DRAWING A PLAN *(continued)*

If you plan to use a sprinkler system, show the direction of prevailing winds, which may affect sprinkler placement. Finally, because you'll have to work around any underground cables, show them as well.

Plan for slope

If the yard is relatively flat, slope is not a concern. If it has a slope of more than 10 percent, however, there could be serious runoff problems if the proper equipment is not used and placed correctly.

In a carefully landscaped yard, most slopes have been eliminated or reduced through terracing and retaining walls. A moderate slope may have been solidified with groundcovers. If any important slopes remain, they need to be measured.

▲ **A sloped area requires special planning to avoid unwanted runoff.**

▼ **Measuring from the topmost point of an incline to its lowest point will allow you to calculate the percentage of slope.**

To measure a slope you need a spirit level or a line level, a long string, a tape measure, and a spike or screwdriver. You might also want an assistant because taking the measurements alone is awkward. Make a loop at one end of the string and attach it to the highest point of ground using a spike or screwdriver sunk into the soil. Have the assistant stand at the bottom of the slope and raise the string, holding it taut, until it is even with the higher ground. Be sure the string is fully horizontal by holding the level against the string or by checking the line level. Let the leftover string fall to the ground from your assistant's hand; a weight attached to one end of the string will help to hold the string taut so that it forms a 90-degree angle.

Now measure both the length of string stretching from the high point of the lot to the assistant's hand and the distance from the assistant's hand to the ground. To find the slope, measured as a percentage, simply divide the rise (measure of height) by the run (measure of length) and multiply by 100.

For example, if the rise is 2 feet and the run is 12 feet, the slope would be approximately 17 percent:

$$2 \div 12 \times 100 = 16.66\%$$

Sketch the slope onto the plan by shading it in with diagonal lines, and indicate the angle of the slope. (If the slope is less than 10 percent, there is no need to show it.)

Divide your yard into zones

Unless your lot is extremely small, you'll need more than one grouping of sprinklers or emitters (each grouping is called a zone) for the front yard and more

MEASURING SLOPE

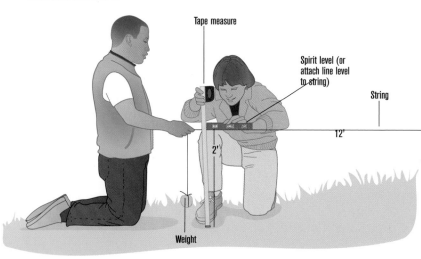

Tape measure

Spirit level (or attach line level to string)

String

12'

2'

Weight

DIVIDING THE PLAN ACCORDING TO WATERING NEEDS

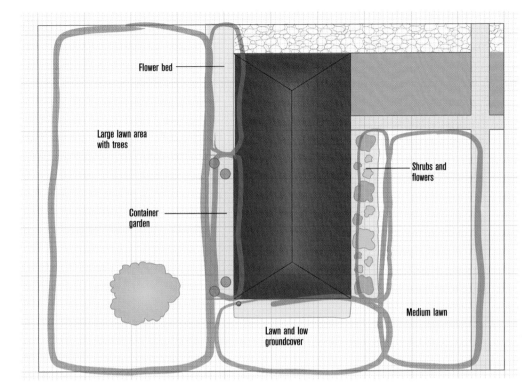

Flower bed

Large lawn area
with trees

Container
garden

Shrubs and
flowers

Medium lawn

Lawn and low
groundcover

than one for the back. The number of zones depends mostly on whether you will use a sprinkler system or microirrigation system (sprinkler systems use more water and, therefore, cover less territory). You will also need to consider the type of sprinkler or emitter you will use and the water requirements of different plants (for example, lawns versus flower beds).

Before deciding how many zones you need, look at your landscape plan and sort plantings into coherent groups, keeping the following points in mind.

Irrigate according to need: Water plants in full sun separately from plants in shade; the former will dry out more quickly.

Turf: Lawns have different watering needs than most other plantings and often require different irrigation equipment. Areas of turf should generally be watered separately.

Deep watering: Plants that require infrequent, deep waterings, such as trees and shrubs, should be watered separately from plants that require frequent, shallow waterings, such as annuals and vegetables.

Coverage: Trees and shrubs planted individually in a lawn can be watered using the lawn system, but take care to ensure they receive adequate moisture from all sides without blocking spray patterns.

▲ **Mark the areas of your lot that will require the same amount and schedule of watering. These will translate into zones controlled by their own valves.**

Scale: In small yards, plantings with similar although not identical needs, such as flower beds, groundcovers, and hedges, can be grouped together. In larger yards where several zones are required anyway, they are best kept separate.

Containers: Plants in containers dry out more quickly than plants in the ground and should be watered separately.

Special needs: Plantings with special needs should be kept separate. Roses, for example, should not have their leaves moistened. If you're using spray irrigation elsewhere, you may prefer to provide a separate microirrigation or bubbler zone for the rose bed. Likewise, Xeriscaped sectors require less water than others and should be watered separately.

Slopes: Problem areas, such as slopes, should be on individual zones.

Taking these factors into account, divide the yard into areas with similar needs. Try to group the areas into squares or rectangles, which are easier to work with than odd-shaped zones. Label the areas according to the predominant vegetation: lawn, shrubs, groundcover. To divide these areas into their final zones according to the type of irrigation and the kinds of sprayers you have chosen, look carefully at the next two chapters on sprinkler irrigation (page 40) and microirrigation (page 72).

ASSESSING GUARANTEES

The materials used in building irrigation systems are increasingly resistant to breakage and damage. Most companies now offer two- to five-year guarantees. Some even have limited lifetime warranties on certain parts.

Commercial-grade products generally cost about one-third more than residential-grade components but are better quality, longer lasting, and less subject to breakage. The guarantee should indicate this.

Product guarantees cover the equipment, not the installation. If you install the system yourself, make sure there are no leaks or breaks. If you hire a contractor, get written guarantees on workmanship, good for at least two years.

SPRINKLER IRRIGATION

For most people, lawn and garden irrigation means an inground sprinkler system. It is by far the most popular method of irrigating residential properties and will undoubtedly remain so. A sprinkler system requires effort to plan and install, but it is not necessarily much more work than a microirrigation system, because there are fewer parts. Once it is up and running, it offers many years of low-maintenance service. The system can be automated so that it practically runs itself.

▼ Sprinkler irrigation can make watering child's play. Planning is the key. The sprinklers on this lawn were sized and placed properly so the spray patterns overlap to ensure an even distribution of water.

In this chapter you'll find specifics about planning and installing a sprinkler system. You'll learn about selecting components, sizing the system, choosing and installing valves, and putting in the system. Read the entire chapter carefully even if you plan to use professional services for certain aspects of your installation, such as planning or trenching. Understanding all aspects of how sprinkler systems operate will help you make important decisions and avoid expensive mistakes.

SELECTING COMPONENTS

An abundance of high-pressure irrigation systems are on the market, each offering a wide range of components. Some companies feature more than fifty different spray head nozzles alone. The basic information here will help direct your choice. First you should understand how inground irrigation works and how to use a system safely.

Choosing the whole ensemble

With an inground sprinkler system, water is carried underground through pipes to individual sprinklers or heads and released under high enough pressure to produce a spray. The coverage of each head varies according to the type of sprinkler, but each one requires a specific amount of pressure. That's why it is important to know the static water pressure for your home's system and the gallons per minute used by each sprinkler head. You can run only so many sprinkler heads before the pressure drops so low the system no longer operates efficiently.

It is always worthwhile to get planning help from an irrigation manufacturer or supplier. Even if your goal is to design and install the system yourself, a supplier with a thorough knowledge of the product line can help you avoid pitfalls.

Whenever possible, purchase products from the same manufacturer, particularly sprinkler heads and components. This is especially true within a given zone. Not only does this ensure parts are compatible, but they will be easier to replace. Parts from the same manufacturer may also be color-coded, an aspect you'll find helpful when you're working with them. As you install the system, write down the name and model number of all the parts and note where in the plan they go. If you need a replacement part, it is easier to pull out your plan than to try to find a tiny serial number stamped on a muddy underground sprinkler housing.

Because they require different pressures to operate effectively, avoid mixing and matching sprinkler types unless the manufacturer suggests it can be done. Bubblers should go on one zone, rotary sprinklers on another, and spray heads on yet another. Full- and part-circle rotary heads can be mixed, as long as you purchase flow-balanced nozzles See page 44. Lawn heads and shrub heads, both spray heads, can be combined. Low- and high-capacity sprinklers need to be on separate zones.

Irrigation systems are constantly being updated. The examples here represent state-of-the-art materials at the time of publication, but don't assume they are still the best or most appropriate. Always check which components are available and the advantages of each before deciding what you need.

▼ **A sampling of sprinkler heads is pictured, *below*. Top row *(left to right)*: Pop-up impact head, pop-up spray head on lateral flex tubing, and gear-driven rotary head. Bottom row: Impact head, spray head on rigid plastic pipe, bubbler on rigid plastic pipe, and stationary spray head on flexible riser.**

PLASTIC OR METAL?

It used to be that all sprinkler parts were made of metal, but that is less and less often the case. Irrigation pipes are now almost always made of plastic and so, increasingly, are sprinkler components. Don't assume that metal parts are necessarily longer lasting or more resistant to breakage or to the elements. Plastic nozzles and pop-up spray heads, for example, are at least as durable as brass ones and often even superior to them, yet are frequently less expensive. If in doubt about whether metal or plastic would be best in your case, consult an irrigation supplier.

SAFETY CONSIDERATIONS

As you design your system, always keep safety in mind. Ensure that risers and pipes do not trip visitors, and prevent damage to your system from garden equipment.

■ **Keep lawn sprinklers low.** One reason why sprinkler irrigation is so popular and safe is that most of its components are underground. There are no hoses or pipes crossing the lawn and walks to cause people to trip. Sprinkler heads can remain level with the ground when not in operation. If above ground, they can be placed in spots where foot traffic is unlikely, such as among shrub plantings and flower beds or along fences and walls. It is especially important to set lawn sprinklers at the right level. In a sea of grass, they are often almost invisible, so any sprinkler even slightly above soil level could cause people to trip.

■ **Keep sprinklers out of harm's way.** Lawn-mower damage can be serious. If a lawn-mower blade hits a sprinkler, not only can the impact break expensive parts, but flying pieces of plastic or metal could harm the mower operator or passersby. Check pop-up heads periodically to make sure they retract efficiently. Place any aboveground parts, such as stationary shrub heads or bubblers, far from danger. If you have doubts about the location of an aboveground part, such as a riser within a bed but only inches from the lawn mower's path, use a swing-joint assembly or attach the riser to flexible pipe (*below*). When bumped, the sprinkler will be pushed out of the way rather than snapped off or broken.

RISER ON FLEXIBLE HOSE

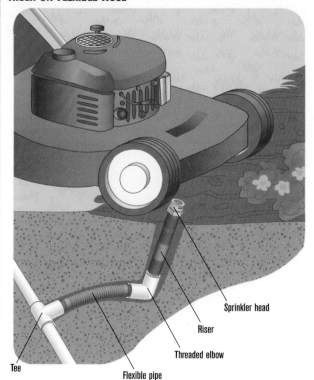

Sprinkler head

Riser

Threaded elbow

Tee

Flexible pipe

■ **Set pipes deep enough.** To assure there is no danger of breakage during any digging, set pipes 8 to 12 inches deep in flower beds and other areas where occasional digging is likely, and even deeper (18 inches) under vegetable beds where digging is a certainty. Do not install pipes in beds where rototillers or other soil-turning equipment are used.

■ **Cover all the valves.** Valves and their numerous connections can present safety problems. Place underground valves in a specially designed inground valve box with the top set flush with the ground (*above*), allowing easy access for repairs or adjustments but creating no danger for passersby or impediment to mowing. The lid should be set firmly on the valve box at all times. Aboveground valve groupings, with various pipes arching in and out of the ground, are especially dangerous. Because they are not visually pleasing, place them in out-of-the-way spots, behind shrubbery, or in a seldom-used corner of the yard. For added safety and to hide valve groupings completely from sight, cover them with a wooden box or shock-resistant container, or place them under a porch or in a toolshed.

■ **Flag danger spots.** Any part of the irrigation system that cannot be placed out of range of foot traffic should be made highly visible with brightly colored reflective paint, a colorful ribbon, or a flag, rather than camouflaged. Be sure to flag danger spots during installation of the system.

■ **Look out for slippery zones.** Excess water is harmful to plants and can create dangerously slippery conditions. Design your sprinkler systems to water lawns and gardens, not walks and driveways. Of course, some overlap is often inevitable, so run the system when foot traffic is unlikely, such as in the early morning. Use nonskid materials for walks that are subject to periodic irrigation spray, especially if the surface is sloped.

Choosing Sprinkler Heads

There is a wide range of sprinkler heads on the market. Take a close look at each of the basic categories—spray, rotary, and bubbler heads—to decide how to plan your system.

Spray heads

These popular, versatile heads produce a broad band of spray in either a full or partial circle, depending on the spray radius you choose. The heads irrigate their entire coverage area at one time. Although they are sometimes called mist heads because their spray can appear mistlike, spray heads actually produce droplets much larger than mist. They cover a moderate radius, usually 8 to 15 feet, so you will need more spray heads than rotary heads to water a given surface. Their smaller range, however, makes them more adaptable than rotary heads.

If you need more than one spray pattern in a zone, look for spray heads with balanced flow, also called flow adjustment or matched precipitation rate. (For more information on sprinkler head spray patterns see pages 50–55.) Balanced flow means the pressure in each is adjusted according to the area it covers. A flow-balanced half-circle head sprays only half as many gallons of water per minute as a full-circle head on the same zone, and a quarter-circle head sprays only one-fourth as much. A quarter-circle head spraying as much water as a full-circle head will have inundated its small area, whereas the full-circle head is just beginning to moisten its sector.

Spray heads can be stationary or pop-up. Both of these categories can further be divided according to their use: flush heads (set level with the soil) and shrub heads (set on risers).

■ **Stationary spray heads:** These have no moving parts to break, making them almost trouble free. Flush stationary heads were once the industry standard for lawns and low groundcovers but are now rarely used. Their major flaw is that the lawn

▲ **Pop-up spray heads are commonly used on medium to small areas.**

▶ **Use flush stationary spray heads only in lawns with short grass.**

▶ **Use stationary shrub heads to water hedges, shrubs, and foundation plantings.**

has to be kept cut short so the spray will not be blocked by tall grasses. Also, in northern climates where most lawn grasses are of the creeping type, the immobility of the spray head leaves it vulnerable to clogging by invasive rhizomes.

Stationary shrub heads are set on risers in order to spray above shrubs, flower beds, groundcovers, and other medium-height vegetation. When the head is set higher than the tallest branch there is no foliage to block the distribution of water. The height is fully adjustable. The riser pipe is cut as needed, taking into account the mature heights of the plants. Shrub heads are usually placed in unobtrusive spots away from foot traffic because their elevated position makes them a safety hazard and susceptible to breakage. To reduce both problems, use a flexible joint at the base of the riser. Shrub heads can use the same type of sprinkler as flush heads, but there are also specially designed shrub sprinkler heads that direct the spray at a lower angle so less water is lost to evaporation.

■ **Pop-up spray heads:** Most lawn sprinkler systems use pop-up heads. Like stationary flush heads, pop-up heads are generally set flush with the soil, but they contain a stem with a nozzle that rises when the water is turned on, then sinks back into the body of the sprinkler when the system is off. The pop-up action allows the heads to reach above nearby plants yet remain unobtrusive

◄ This pop-up spray head is adjusted to deliver a direct spray over a quarter- to half-circle area.

◄ Rotary heads are designed to send out strong streams of water over long distances.

when not in use. Pop-up heads are most popular for lawns and low-growing groundcovers, but taller models can be used with small shrubs, vegetation of moderate height, and annuals. Pop-up heads can also be put on risers for use with tall shrubs.

Pop-up heads are available in various heights, ranging from 1 to 12 inches. If you're looking for a specific height, especially among the taller models, make sure the manufacturer you choose carries them. For short-mown lawns, 2-inch or even 1-inch pop-up heads are perfectly acceptable, but for the typical 3-inch-tall lawn, 3-inch or 4-inch heads are more appropriate.

Although water pressure pushes the pop-up nozzle out of its casing, gravity is not always sufficient to retract it. That's why pop-up sprayers of more than 2 inches in height are generally spring-loaded. Both gravity nozzles and spring-loaded nozzles contain few moving parts that are subject to breakage. Both are designed to keep out dirt because soil particles can clog the pop-up action. If the nozzles become clogged, however, you can easily take them apart for cleaning.

GETTING THE PIPE SIZES RIGHT

Landscape-quality pipes in both PVC and poly, or polyethylene, are available in various sizes; the most common are ¾ inch, 1 inch, and 1¼ inch. Valves also come with variously sized openings. Be sure to get pipes and valves large enough for your needs; if you don't, your sprinklers will not be able to do their job.

Contrary to what many people think, stepping down in pipe size decreases water pressure rather than increasing it. In some cases you may want to move from a smaller to a larger diameter pipe. For instance, you may choose to install 1¼-inch pipe even if your service line is only 1 inch.

Take the following factors into account when choosing pipe size: the total number of gallons used by the sprinkler heads, the total length of your pipes, the type of pipe, the number of elbows used, and elevation changes.

Your best bet is to take all your plans to a qualified irrigation dealer, who can tell you what size pipe to use.

Rotary heads

Also known as stream heads, rotary heads cover the largest area of any sprinkler. Rather than supplying a sheet of water and irrigating their entire sector at once, rotary heads send out a high-velocity stream of water in one or two directions, then rotate slowly to cover the entire area. Because only part of the surface is irrigated at any one time, the flow is concentrated, allowing the rotary head to throw water much farther than a spray head can. Most rotary heads cover a minimum radius of 16 to 22 feet and a maximum of 40 to 48 feet, considerably more than the range of 8 to 15 feet for a spray head.

Because it is difficult to design a nozzle that can simultaneously spray an area 45 feet from the head and the area within a few feet of its base, rotary heads usually have two nozzles: a long-range nozzle for the outer limits of its area and a short-range nozzle for the inner part. In part-circle heads, both nozzles point in the same direction, giving the impression of a solid stream that waters from the head to the outer limits of its coverage area. Some short-range rotary heads have only one nozzle, because the area they cover efficiently falls within the range of one nozzle.

Rotary heads apply water more slowly than do high-gallonage spray heads, a boon for slow-to-drain clay soils. However, this means they need to run about four times longer than spray heads, which can cause problems in areas with water restrictions. Rotary heads lose more water to evaporation than spray heads do. On the positive side,

▲ **An antibacksplash device protects neighbors and passersby from stray spray.**

you will need fewer rotary heads than spray heads to cover a given space.

Individually, rotary heads are less efficient than spray heads, but because you use fewer of them, a system with rotaries will usually waste less water than a system with spray heads. If your area is subject to strong winds, rotaries will waste more water because the water from them is more susceptible to being blown off course and to evaporating.

Rotary heads are very popular in public parks but less so in residential areas. Few homes have the large expanses of unobstructed lawn or groundcover that rotary heads water so efficiently. Full-circle heads, which typically cover a minimum

	THE BEST SPRINKLER FOR YOUR NEEDS				
	SPRAY HEADS		ROTARY HEADS		
	Lawn head	Shrub head	Impact or gear	Multistream	Bubblers
Small lawns	Yes	No	No	No	No
Medium lawns	Yes	No	Yes	Yes	No
Large lawns	Sometimes	No	Yes	Sometimes	No
Flower beds	No	Yes	No	No	Yes
Groundcovers	Low ones	Yes	Low ones	Low ones	Yes
Shrubs	No	Yes	No	No	Yes
Isolated areas	No	No	No	No	Yes
Slopes	Low gallonage	Low gallonage	Yes	Yes	No

diameter of 40 feet, are poorly suited for an average home landscape, but half- and quarter-circle rotary heads placed against walls or fences or in corners can be useful for large square or rectangular lawn.

Rotary heads can be either pop-up or stationary. Stationary rotary heads on risers of varying height are used on the periphery of large to medium lawns and planting areas. Pop-up rotary heads installed flush with the ground are usually set into lawns.

Impact sprinklers: The best known and most frequently used rotary head is the impact drive, or impulse sprayer. It uses a spring-loaded drive arm that, when pulled into the stream of water by the spring, is deflected sideways, giving a jerky rotational movement and that familiar sh-sh-sh sound. Most impact sprinklers are almost fully adjustable and can cover a full circle or any part of one. For part-circle use, look for impact heads with a built-in antibacksplash device to keep them from watering sectors you want kept dry.

Metal impact heads generally require a minimum static water pressure of 40 psi to operate efficiently. If your system has a static water pressure of 40 psi or less, use plastic impact heads.

Gear-driven sprinklers: Gear-driven pop-up rotary heads are becoming more popular. They include a series of gears that drive the rotary stream in a smooth and nearly noiseless pattern. The gears are hidden in an underground casing. Choose one with a closed-case design, which keeps out dirt. Most gear-driven drives are fully adjustable from full- to partial-circle patterns and cover about the same surface as impact heads.

Multistream rotors: Producing several streams that rotate slowly to cover their entire trajectory, spray from multistream rotors doesn't reach as far as from other stream rotors. Multistream rotors cover more surface than spray heads and are best reserved for intermediate surfaces, from about 16 to 31 feet wide. There are both shrub sprinkler rotors and pop-up lawn sprinklers in this category. They are usually adaptable to full- and part-circle needs through interchangeable nozzles.

▼ **Multistream rotary heads produce fingerlike streams of water and rotate slowly to cover their entire spray zone.**

SPRAY PATTERNS

Sprinkler heads of all types (spray, rotary, and bubbler) are available in different patterns, the best known of which is the full circle. But half-circle and quarter-circle patterns are just as useful because they allow you to place sprinklers on the periphery of the zone they will irrigate, out of the way of lawn mowers and foot traffic, rather than in the center. Three-quarter, two-third, and one-third patterns are also available, as are heads with adjustable spray patterns, often called VAN heads.

Special spray-pattern nozzles for specific uses include strip nozzles used to water long, narrow strips such as parkways or narrow raised beds. They come in four patterns: square, center, side, and end. Center strip sprinklers spray in two directions at once. Side strip sprinklers also water

in two directions but are placed along the edge of the strip. End strip sprinklers water in only one direction. The square strip sprinkler is designed for wider strips; it waters in all four directions from its center placement.

| Full circle | ¾ circle | ⅔ circle | ½ circle | ⅓ circle | ¼ circle |

| Square strip | Center strip | Side strip | End strip |

Bubblers

The bubbler, or flood head, is related to the spray head but is designed to deliver a large quantity of water to a relatively small area, usually up to a circumference of about 5 feet. The name bubbler comes from the sound the water makes as it gushes out of the head. Bubblers should be raised high enough from the ground (usually about

▼ **Bubblers soak the soil around them, covering only a small surface. They are usually used for shrubs and groundcovers.**

4 to 6 inches) so they won't get clogged. Most are adjustable to emit anything from a full flow to a light trickle. Most are full-circle heads, but some offer part-circle functions. Bubblers are useful for small areas of medium-height vegetation. Because they water only the soil and not the foliage, they are an ideal choice for plants such as roses, which won't tolerate water on their leaves. However, they make poor choices for sandy soils, because they operate by flooding the surrounding area. In sandy soil this means the excess water drains away without reaching nearby plants. Place bubblers on separate zones and, because they deliver water rapidly to a small surface, run them only for short periods. Bubbler heads are increasingly being replaced by microsprinklers. See page 79 for more information on microsprinklers.

LOW-GALLONAGE HEADS

Unless otherwise specified by the manufacturer, you can assume sprinklers are of standard gallonage and designed for normal water pressure.

Low-gallonage heads are intended for areas where water pressure is moderate to low (a static water pressure of less than 40 psi) or where water conservation is a priority. Because they apply water at a slower rate than other sprinklers, they are ideal where the soil is mostly clay and subject to runoff. Some companies call these sprinklers low-pressure heads, a term better reserved for microirrigation applications, which operate at even lower pressure.

CHOOSING PIPING MATERIALS

Although your home may have galvanized steel or copper piping, and municipal regulations may require the use of copper piping right up to the backflow preventer, irrigation piping is almost always made of plastic. It does not corrode over time, is low in cost, and is easy to install. The two products currently in use are rigid PVC piping and flexible polyethylene piping (poly pipe). Each has its advantages; many irrigation systems use both.

PVC pipe

PVC (polyvinyl chloride) is practically unbreakable; landscape-quality PVC pipe is usually rated at 160 psi or better, making it very resistant to bursting. It is relatively unaffected by temperature change and is unlikely to be damaged by expansion and contraction in all but the coldest climates when placed at an appropriate depth. PVC is usually more expensive than poly pipe and will need more joints because it lacks flexibility. Each joint must be welded individually using a solvent, making installation time-consuming. In winter, PVC pipes must be drained so that ice doesn't form and crack the pipe as it expands. PVC pipe is available in various lengths, but 20 feet is standard. Schedule 40 PVC is usually recommended for outdoor irrigation. Do not use leftover PVC from indoor use.

Polyethylene pipe

Polyethylene, or poly, pipe is rapidly taking the place of PVC as the pipe of choice for home-irrigation systems. It is flexible and,

▲ **Almost all residential irrigation systems use polyethylene or PVC pipe.**

▼ **Poly pipe connections usually call for easy-to-install clamps.**

as a result, easier to install. You can bend it slightly to go around obstacles instead of having to cut the pipe and add extra joints. Connections are easily made without messy solvents. In many cases you can even avoid trenching by using pipe-pulling equipment. Poly pipe is sold in coils of various lengths. Use only landscape-quality poly pipe with an appropriate pressure rating. Poly pipe marked "NSF" is of guaranteed uniform quality, while "non-NSF" pipe may have inconsistent wall thicknesses.

Poly pipe does have two major flaws. When digging in the garden, you can slice through the pipe without knowing you've done so. Bury poly pipe at least 8 inches deep to avoid problems. Also, its strength is limited. Over time, pressure surges can weaken poly pipe and cause it to crack. This can lead to the pipe bursting under high pressure. Poly pipe is best suited for use downstream of the valves.

PVC and polyethylene together

There is no clear-cut answer whether PVC or poly pipe is the better choice. Some people prefer to use PVC throughout their system, trusting in its superior strength and durability. Increasingly, manufacturers suggest a combination of the two.

Pressure surges are likely to occur only in the main pipes, not in the zones. You can use PVC for the supply lines leading to each zone, and use poly pipe to link the sprinklers within each zone. In areas where freezing can occur to depths up to 12 inches, rigid PVC pipe can pull apart as it contracts. Poly pipe, however, is compressed by the weight of soil in such deep installations. In these circumstances some irrigation experts recommend using only metal pipe where a pressure surge is possible and, elsewhere, using loosely installed poly pipe inserted inside larger-diameter PVC pipe. The loose installation of the poly pipe means it can contract in cold weather, while the surrounding PVC pipe protects it from compression. Obviously, double piping is expensive.

SIZING THE SPRINKLER SYSTEM

Now that you've sketched a simple plan and gathered the basic information about your home, yard, and water capacity as well as the type of sprinklers and piping you intend to use, it is time to plot sprinkler locations on your plan.

Plotting an irrigation plan

Ideally you should take the information you've gathered and the plot plan to an expert, who will produce a precise irrigation plan. If you intend to plot the plan on your own, have a specialist look it over and point out errors. Many will do so for free or for a modest fee. Another option is to use a manufacturer's free online or mail-order planning service. It is better to ask a specialist's advice now, even if you have to pay for it, than to spend hundreds of dollars later in renovations because of a faulty plan. In particular it is important to get your pipe sizes right. For more information on sizing pipes see page 45.

To plot the plan yourself, you'll need a calculator, colored pencils, an eraser, a lead pencil, the manufacturer's equipment chart or list, a pencil compass, a ruler, and your plan. It is important to have a copy of the manufacturer's equipment chart. You'll need it to determine the minimum and maximum spacing, the flow in gpm, and the spray pattern for each sprinkler. These charts are usually divided according to the type of sprinkler (spray head, rotary, or bubbler) and include a list of valves, fittings, timers, and other parts.

GETTING SPACING RIGHT

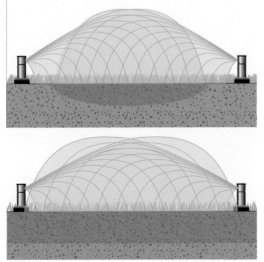

► Incorrect spacing *(top)* creates areas that are over- and underwatered. Proper head-to-head coverage ensures even water distribution within each zone *(bottom)*.

Your plan should already show the buildings, plantings, walks, and other landscape elements. You should also have divided up the plantings into roughly square or rectangular areas according to type (lawns, shrub borders, groundcovers); this is the basis of your plan for different irrigation zones.

To begin, draw in the sprinkler heads and calculate whether the water capacity in each sector is sufficient.

Overlapping spray patterns

To irrigate adequately, spray patterns must overlap. Water loses force as it leaves the sprinkler head and may not reach the outer edge of the spray pattern sufficiently. If only one sprinkler covers an area, the center will get more water than the outer areas. Also the perimeter of a spray pattern is apt to be disrupted by winds.

Avoid dry spots and other problems by spacing sprinkler heads so that water from one head reaches adjacent spray heads; this is known as head-to-head coverage. For example, sprinkler heads that have a spray diameter of 30 feet (and therefore a radius or throw of 15 feet) should be 15 feet apart. (The distance a sprinkler can propel water is called a "throw.") In windy areas, it helps to space heads closer together—up to 90 percent of the throw—to compensate for distortion to the spray pattern. For example, sprinklers with 15-foot throws should be spaced 13½ feet apart.

You can adjust most spray heads to spray a radius of 10 to 15 feet; the average rotary sprayer covers a radius of 25 to 45 feet; most bubblers reach 1 to 5 feet. If your static water pressure is lower than normal (40 psi or less), choose a smaller radius as the appropriate spacing. The manufacturer's charts will indicate the proper minimum and maximum spacing for each sprinkler.

Plotting sprinkler placement

Plot sprinkler heads using a pencil compass adjusted to the appropriate spacing. If you're using 1 foot to one square on your graph paper and the sprinklers you're using have a throw of 10 feet, adjust the compass to a 10-square distance (10 feet). To cover the greatest surface with the fewest number of sprinklers, first use the maximum recommended spacing (less if the site is windy or if water pressure is lower than normal). If the area cannot be divided evenly, place sprinklers closer together.

TRIANGULAR AND SQUARE SPACING

Irrigation plans are usually drawn using either square spacing or triangular (staggered) spacing. Square spacing, with heads located at each of the four corners, is the easiest to plot. There is, however, excessive overlap because some spots inevitably are watered by four sprinklers. Also, because sprinklers have to be placed relatively close (usually at 50 percent of the diameter or throw), more sprinkler heads are needed (the illustration *below* shows this). In triangular spacing, heads are located at each of the three points formed by a triangle. This means more surface is covered with less overlap, heads can be placed farther apart (usually at 60 percent of the diameter or throw, or even slightly more), and fewer heads are needed. For example, spray heads are typically placed at 15 feet or less in square spacing, 20 feet for triangular spacing.

To plot triangular spacing, first choose one side of a rectangular or square area as a baseline, then plot the two corner quarter-circle sprinklers, followed by equidistant half-circle sprinklers in between them as needed (so far, this is the same as square spacing). Next draw lines upward from the center points between the sprinklers. Place the next row of sprinklers, not on the main line, as in square spacing, but at the half-space line. Continue to alternate the sprinkler heads between half-space and full-space lines. This will give you a triangular spacing. You may have some overshoot on the outside edges, but this water loss is compensated by the system's greater efficiency.

PLACING SPRINKLER HEADS

Square Spacing (more heads are needed for complete coverage)

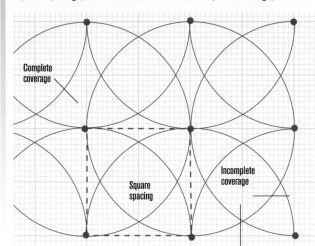

Triangular Spacing (complete coverage shown)

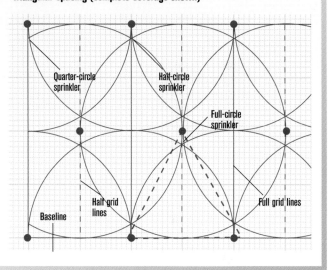

Begin plotting in the four corners of the squares and rectangles you drew on your plan, drawing a quarter circle in each. Position sprinklers evenly along the sides, drawing a half circle around each. If this placement doesn't cover the entire area, place sprinklers in the center and draw a full circle around each. Each circle should almost touch the head next to it. This will give you equidistant, or square, spacing. See the box *above* for the more complex but more efficient triangular spacing.

▌ **Step-by-step planning:** Start with the largest of the squares or rectangles on your plan, leaving the smaller and odd-shaped sections for last. When you've completed the larger rectangles, position heads in small lawn areas, such as parking strips. These are usually watered by one or two rows of partial circles. Water narrow spaces with strip nozzles (for lawns) or bubblers (for shrubs, beds, or groundcovers).

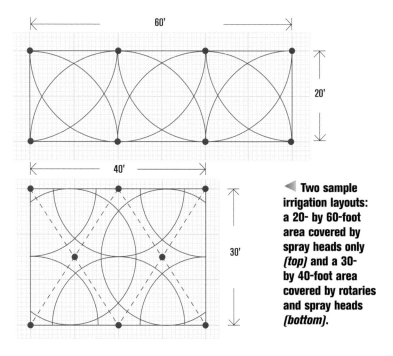

◀ **Two sample irrigation layouts: a 20- by 60-foot area covered by spray heads only *(top)* and a 30- by 40-foot area covered by rotaries and spray heads *(bottom).***

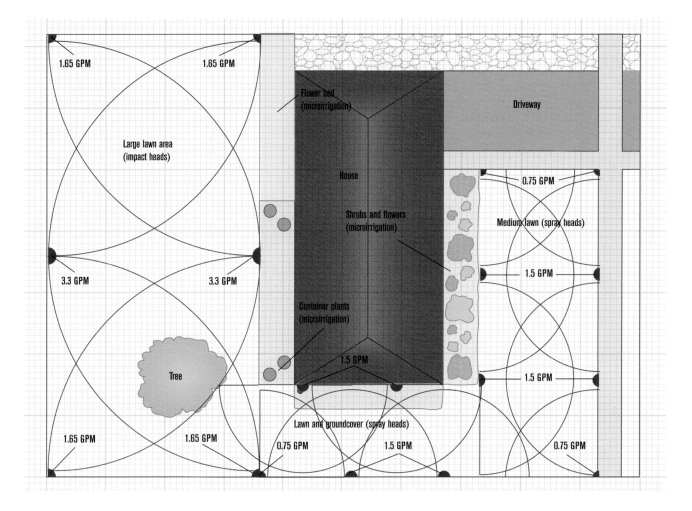

Finally, add sufficient shrub spray heads and bubblers to irrigate shrub areas, flower beds, and planters. Set the sprinklers, where possible, at the back of the bed or along the periphery.

As you position sprinklers, jot down the details you'll need later to determine the zones. As you draw circles and part circles indicating spray trajectory, show the placement of the head with a dot. Whole dots can indicate full-circle heads, and half or quarter dots can indicate half-circle and quarter-circle heads. Show the gpm rating for each sprinkler. You can find gpm ratings on the manufacturer's chart.

Special layout techniques

Home landscapes rarely fit perfectly into equidistant sprinkler plans. You may have areas that need special planning. Here are ideas for coping with nonstandard elements.

▓ **Adjustable pattern heads:** Rotary heads are generally fully adjustable, but most spray heads have fixed spray patterns: full circle, three-quarter circle, half circle, etc. If you

have an awkward angle, consider using adjustable pattern heads (VANs). Most adjust from 1 degree to 330 degrees.

▓ **Fill-in heads:** In many cases equally spaced layout patterns cover most of a zone, but leave a few spots underwatered. Rather than struggling to design a perfect match, add a fill-in head. This fill-in sprinkler either is not located in the same symmetrical pattern as the others or has a smaller or greater coverage than the others. Sometimes such heads cause significant overlap, but this is better than leaving dry spots.

▓ **Undesirable overthrow:** Most homeowners have areas they want to keep dry, such as public sidewalks, yet some overthrow is inevitable, especially with triangular spacing. To keep a space spray-free use it as the baseline for your triangular layout. With a combination of quarter- and half-circle heads, you can usually design the first line without overshoot. If you have two lines in the same sector where overthrow cannot be allowed (such as on a corner lot where two sidewalks intersect), you may need to modify the basic pattern with fill-in heads and part-circle nozzles.

■ **Obstacles:** One common problem is ensuring water reaches all parts of the garden in spite of obstacles. Even a flagpole can block enough spray to leave a dry zone on its far side. A triangular spacing of sprinkler heads with the obstacle at the approximate center of throw solves the problem nicely. When trees and other obstacles do not fall at the desired point of junction in an otherwise equidistant spray area, try adjusting the plotting; however, you will probably need fill-in heads with smaller ranges.

Similarly, groups of obstacles, such as clusters of shrubs, can be watered by outside heads positioned around them in a triangular pattern. Make sure that all spots are reached by at least part of the trajectory.

Remember that trees and shrubs in lawns need more water than grass. You might want to put them on a separate zone, provide them with microirrigation, or resort to occasional hand watering.

■ **Rounded corners and curves:** It is difficult to avoid overthrow at rounded corners, such as the curved entrance to a driveway, but you can reduce overthrow with careful placement of sprinkler heads or use of adjustable heads. Curves are also difficult, but overlap is preferable to dry spots. The illustrations at *right* show various ways of using half-circle sprinklers to irrigate inside and outside curves.

■ **Hedges and borders:** Shrubs, flower beds, and hedges are best watered on their own zones with bubblers, shrub heads, or microirrigation, but they can be irrigated with flush heads placed on their periphery that can also water the lawn. If the hedge or planting is dense enough, water will not pass through it to soak the wall behind or the property next door.

Dividing into zones

Once your landscape plan has spray trajectories well indicated, and all surfaces will receive adequate coverage, it is time to divide the plan into proper zones.

Except in small lots the operating pressure for your property will not allow you to run all sprinklers at once, and even if it did, you probably wouldn't want to. After all you won't want a shady lawn that stays relatively moist to be watered as often as a planter box in full sun. This is why the plan has to be divided into individual zones, each with a total operating pressure

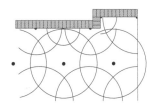

Working around a building

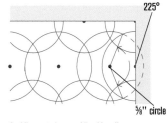

225°

⅝" circle

Avoiding watering a public sidewalk

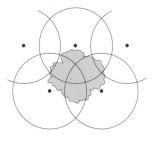

Using triangular spacing to work around an obstacle

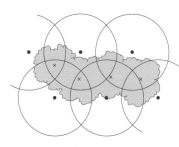

Using triangular spacing for an irregular group planting

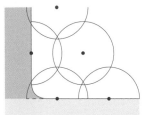

Reducing water loss at a rounded corner

Watering hedges and lawns with a sprinkler on a riser

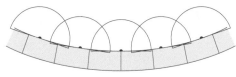

Irrigating around inside and outside rounded corners

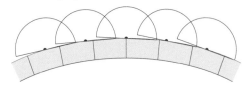

no greater than the system can support. Each zone contains a varying number of sprinkler heads that operate together off a common valve.

Earlier when you grouped the areas of the yard according to plant type and type of sprinkler required, then sketched in the sprinkler heads, you laid the groundwork for zoning. Just remember that each zone must contain only heads of the same type (rotary, spray, or bubbler). After that, simply verify that the zones don't contain more

DIVIDING A PLAN INTO CIRCUITS

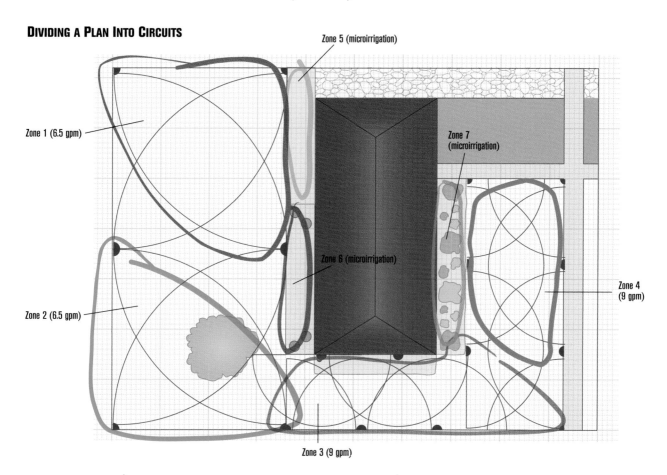

Zone 5 (microirrigation)

Zone 1 (6.5 gpm)

Zone 7 (microirrigation)

Zone 6 (microirrigation)

Zone 4 (9 gpm)

Zone 2 (6.5 gpm)

Zone 3 (9 gpm)

sprinkler heads than the available pressure will allow.

To check this add the gpm of all the sprinklers on each potential zone, then add 10 percent (pressure loss due to pipe length and other factors) and compare this total with the capacity of your system (maximum gpm flow per zone) that you found by using the tables on page 35. For example, if the total gpm of the sprinkler heads on a proposed zone is 9, add .9 gpm (10 percent), for a total of 9.9 gpm. If your maximum gpm is 12, you can use the zone as is. If the sum is 15 gpm plus 1.5, giving you a total of 16.5 gpm, divide the zone into two. In borderline cases, be safe and divide the zone.

As you determine the zones, take into account any future plans. If you intend to add a flower bed or a few containers, leave some extra capacity in nearby zones.

Locating valves and lines

Once zones are established on paper, it is time to determine a path for bringing in water to supply the sprinkler heads. Start by plotting the water meter and the main service line on the plan. You've already located the water meter. The main service line usually follows a straight line from the water meter to the street if the water meter is indoors, or between the water meter and the point where the water line enters the house if the meter is located near the street. Show the main service line on the plan as a dotted line.

■ **Main irrigation shutoff valve location:** Now determine where you'll be installing the main irrigation shutoff valve. This manual valve, used to turn the entire irrigation system on and off, should be installed on the house side of the water meter. It will be either outdoors at some point between the meter and the house or in the basement. In nonfreezing climates and under certain

---

DON'T FORGET

If you have to subdivide a proposed zone, consider the following factors:

■ Plants with similar needs should be irrigated together.

■ Certain parts of the lawn may be shadier and need less irrigation.

■ If your yard is hilly, sprinklers that are at about the same elevation should be grouped together; otherwise, the water in the system will drain out through the lowest sprinkler each time the sprinkler is turned off, possibly causing flooding.

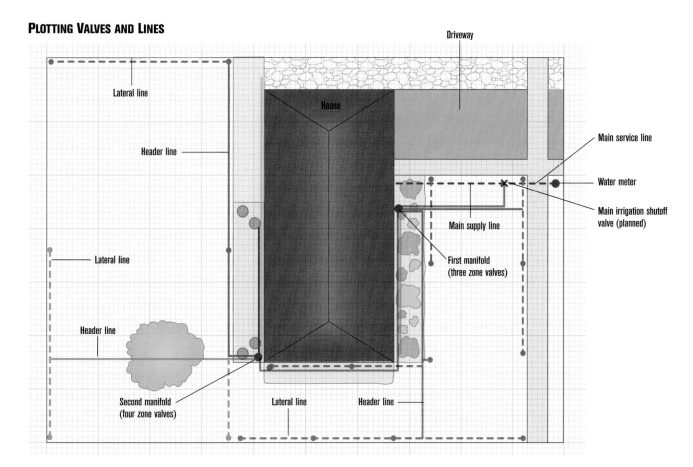

circumstances, you may also be able to install the main irrigation shutoff valve from an outside faucet. See page 60 to determine whether this is appropriate for your situation. Mark the planned main irrigation shutoff valve location on your irrigation plan.

Zone control-valve locations: Each zone will be operated by a separate control valve. Group these together in an accessible spot outdoors, such as near a door or patio but away from heavy foot traffic. Each group of valves is called a manifold, or valve grouping. In most cases it is practical to have two manifolds, one for the front yard and one for the back and side yards.

To simplify installation, plan to put one manifold near the main service line. If you use outdoor faucet lines as a hookup, locate the manifolds near them. Mark the manifolds on your plan.

Plotting the main supply line: Next determine the path of the main supply line that will link the two manifolds to the main irrigation shutoff valve. Mark this line on your plan. If your main irrigation shutoff valve will be located indoors, run the line outdoors first, then in opposite directions, one line leading toward the first manifold and the other around the house to the second manifold. If the shutoff is near the street, run the main supply line first toward the house, then toward the manifolds.

Plotting the irrigation pipes: Because each zone has a separate control valve, plot an irrigation pipe system for each. Start by drawing one header line per zone. This main line will carry water to the lateral lines, so be sure not to connect sprinkler heads to it. To each header line, add lateral lines as needed to connect the sprinkler heads on that zone. The following tips will help you plan:

▨ Avoid forcing water to travel through too many turns; pressure will be lost.

▨ Avoid directing lines under established driveways and sidewalks.

▨ Mark each zone with a different color.

▨ Place header lines side by side so they can share a trench whenever possible to reduce digging.

▨ Place lines 1 or 2 feet outside established flower beds and shrub plantings to avoid damaging roots when digging the trenches.

▨ Plot lines about 3 feet from the house and other structures to avoid damaging pipes.

PUTTING IT ALL TOGETHER

Now that your plan is drawn up, it's time to get organized. Prepare a parts list, stake out the yard, and gather your tools and materials.

Preparing a parts list

If an irrigation professional planned the system, this step is done: A list of parts will be included with the plot plan. If you've done the work on your own, you can still take the plan to a specialist who can calculate your needs. If no help is available, go over your plan carefully, measuring the length of both poly pipe and PVC pipe, and calculating the number of heads, couplings, tees, and clamps. You'll also need materials for tying into your household water system, control valves, and other components described on pages 58–68.

Most irrigation suppliers offer parts lists with blank spaces that you can fill in to indicate the number of each of the items you need. Use a pencil—you'll inevitably make changes.

▼ **Colored flags, available at home centers, nurseries, and irrigation supply outlets, help you to differentiate zones when staking out an irrigation system.**

Staking out your yard

Before gathering materials, transfer your plan from paper to your yard. Use wood stakes or flags (an irrigation supplier should offer the latter in a variety of colors). If possible, color-code markers according to the colors on your plan, and mark the name of the part on each marker to avoid confusion.

First stake out the main supply line, water meter, manifold locations, and valve positions. Then place markers for the header lines and lateral lines and, finally, each of the sprinkler heads.

Check the spacing of sprinkler heads by cutting a length of string to represent the proposed radius or throw, nailing or tying it to the stake or flag representing the sprinkler head, then walking the circle holding the string to see where water will reach. Its spray should touch or nearly touch neighboring heads. Make any necessary adjustments.

Now run string from the stakes to indicate the paths of the pipes. Doing so might well show places where you can use common trenches to save some digging or reveal overlooked obstacles. Finally, if you'll be using automatic controls (see page 98), stake out a trench leading from the main control valves to the system timer box, usually located in a garage, basement, or other protected area.

Gathering materials and tools

You will need these essential tools, *opposite,* for laying out and installing your sprinkler system. In addition you may need a shovel, rake, and hoe. Also shown are the tools you'll need to tie into a galvanized-steel or copper supply line; your situation may not require all of them.

Wear eye protection when cutting metal or concrete and ear protection when using motorized tools. Installing irrigation is a ground-level task; knee pads make the job much more comfortable.

You also will need to have on hand supplies and materials such as electrical tape, waterproof connectors, 1-inch pipe clamps for poly pipe, pipe plugs, PVC primer and cement, pipe joint tape, dry rags, sand, gravel, and wooden stakes.

If the water hookup is in the basement and you will have to drill through the foundation wall for your supply line, you'll also need two-part plumber's epoxy or hydraulic cement.

INSTALLATION TOOLS AND SUPPLIES

50-foot tape measure

Mattock

Phillips/standard screwdriver

Marker flags

12-foot tape measure

Plastic-pipe cutters

Layout string

Pipe wrench

Pliers

Groove-joint pliers

Adjustable wrench

Crimper

Torpedo level

Propane torch, lighter

Power drill

Masonry bit

Pipe cleaning tool

Tubing cutter

Hack saw

PVC saw

Utility knife

PIPE FITTINGS

Pipe fittings for irrigation systems include a bewildering array of small parts. These are among the common ones.

POLY PIPE

•**Insert Coupling:** Connects two lengths of poly pipe.

•**Insert Tee:** Connects three lengths of poly pipe.

•**Combination Tee:** Attaches threaded riser between poly pipe and sprinkler.

•**Insert Elbow:** Forms 90° angle using two pieces of poly pipe.

•**Combination Elbow:** Forms 90° angle using poly pipe and PVC pipe.

•**Insert Adapter:** Adapts threaded outlet to insert fitting for poly pipe.

•**Stainless-Steel Clamp:** Clamps insert fittings.

PVC PIPE

•**Threaded Coupling:** Connects sprinklers to ½" riser.

•**Slip or Socket Coupling:** Connects two lengths of same size PVC pipe.

•**Reducer Bushing:** Connects two lengths of different size PVC pipe.

•**Slip or Socket Tee:** Connects same size PVC pipe at 90° from main line.

•**Reducer Tee:** Attaches threaded riser between PVC pipe and sprinkler.

•**90° Slip or Socket Elbow:** Forms 90° angle with same size PVC pipe.

•**45° Slip or Socket Elbow:** Forms 45° angle with same size PVC pipe.

•**Reducer Elbow:** Forms 90° angle and provides threads for threaded riser.

•**Male Adapter:** Adapts threaded outlet to socket for joint PVC pipe.

BOTH POLY AND PVC PIPE

•**Manifold Tee:** Connects control valves together into manifold.

•**Threaded Riser:** Rises from pipe to sprinkler.

•**Cutoff Riser:** Rises from pipe to sprinkler. Can be cut to desired height.

•**Adjustable Riser:** Rises from pipe to sprinkler. Height can be adjusted.

•**Flexible Riser:** Rises from pipe to sprinkler in high-traffic areas. Flexible.

•**Drain Cap:** Cap for draining system.

•**Drain Valve:** Automatically drains system when pressure is off.

•**Slip-Type Compression Tee:** Connects irrigation system to main service line.

•**Inground Valve Box:** Protects underground valves.

INSTALLING THE SYSTEM

Give yourself plenty of time to install your irrigation system. It's better to work slowly and carefully than to rush and make mistakes.

Each step of the installation should be done with the water turned off. Turn it off at the meter in the beginning stages and later at the main irrigation shutoff valve. After each step, turn on the water to check for leaks and to flush the system.

Tying into your water supply

How you hook the irrigation system to the local water main depends on where your water meter is located. If you don't have a water meter, tie into the system after the shutoff valve for the main service line. Locate the cut as close as you can to the planned location of the backflow preventer (see page 63). To ensure proper pipe sizing, see page 45.

Your home's water line, proceeding from the meter, is made of galvanized steel, copper, or PVC. Each type of pipe requires a slightly different method for adding a tee fitting. In most cases you'll use a transition fitting that lets you join schedule 40 PVC pipe—the pipe used in most irrigation systems—to your home's steel or copper line.

Before you break into the main supply line, turn off the water to your home. Shut off the valve on the house side of the water meter. Your shutoff may be in the outdoor "buffalo box" that holds your meter. In rare cases, you'll have to call your water department to turn off the water. After you have shut off the water, open the taps in your house to let the water remaining in the pipes drain out. When you're ready to cut into the pipe, have a bucket handy if you are working where spills are a concern.

Working with steel, copper, or PVC pipe

While it is best to make the transition to PVC as soon as possible, you may find you have to tie into or extend your existing supply line before you can do so. One general rule: At each threaded connection, apply pipe-thread tape or pipe compound. This will make the pipes fit together more easily and help create a better seal.

Here are some pointers on working with the types of pipe you'll find.

■ **Galvanized steel:** Pipe threads go in only one direction, so you cannot remove a pipe in the middle of a run. You must cut into it and, with the help of a fitting called a union, install your tee and rebuild the section of pipe removed. You may need a new piece of pipe threaded to suit your situation. Often a stock piece of pipe (the shorter ones are known as nipples) will fit. If you use copper in your watering system, make the transition from steel to copper with a fitting called a dielectric union to avoid corrosion. For more on working with galvanized steel pipe, see page 61.

■ **Copper:** Although a sweat joint is more permanent (see page 62), a compression fitting can be used safely with copper. Always cut copper with a tubing cutter; a hacksaw will dent the pipe out of round. You may have to sweat a cap onto a piece of pipe to temporarily seal off the tee.

■ **PVC:** Although PVC may have enough give in it to cement a tee in place, a compression tee (*below*) is easier. Have a capped piece of pipe ready to temporarily seal off the tee. For more on working with PVC, see page 64.

Common hookups

On the following page are three of the most common main-line connections. The instructions assume you are using schedule 40 PVC pipe for this part of the system and that you are doing the work yourself. Some municipalities may require copper or metal

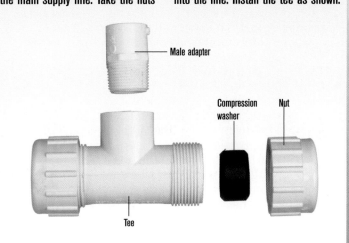

PVC TEE

PVC is one of the easiest types of pipe to tie into. Purchase a PVC compression tee to suit the dimension of the main supply line. Take the nuts off the tee, hold the tee in place, and mark for your cuts. Use a plastic-pipe saw or other fine-toothed saw to cut into the line. Install the tee as shown.

Male adapter

Compression washer

Nut

Tee

INSTALLING THE SYSTEM *(continued)*

TYPES OF WATER HOOKUPS

HOOKING UP NEAR AN OUTSIDE METER

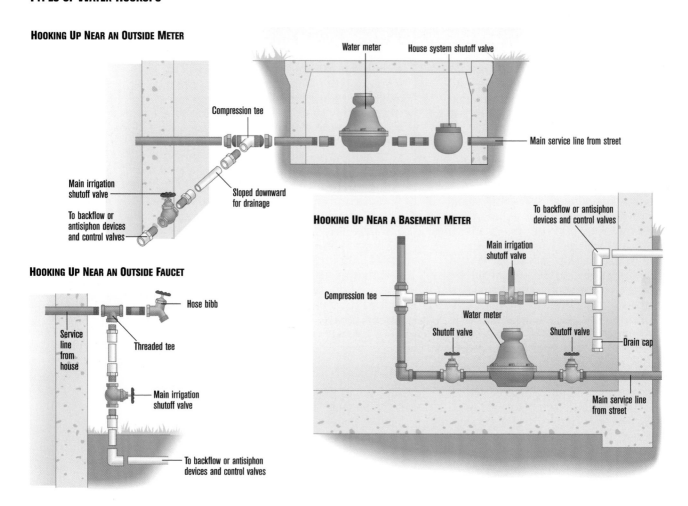

HOOKING UP NEAR AN OUTSIDE FAUCET

HOOKING UP NEAR A BASEMENT METER

▲ **These are some of the common arrangements for tying an irrigation system into your water system.**

piping and may also insist that a licensed plumber handle this stage. Because codes vary, check them before installing any system.

■ **Hooking up near an outside meter:** Turn off the water supply at the meter. Cut into the service line between the meter and the house, wherever it is most convenient. That may be near the street or near where the service line enters the house, depending on where you plan to install the first manifold. Using a tubing cutter for copper or a hacksaw (see *facing page*) for galvanized pipe, cut into the main service line. Add a tee of an appropriate diameter (¾ inch, 1 inch, or 1¼ inch, depending on the size of the pipe). With galvanized steel pipe you will need a union as well. Using a short section of PVC pipe, install a valve to act as the main irrigation shutoff valve. For easier access place the valve in an inground valve box. Now connect the main supply line and run it to the first manifold. Turn on

the water at the meter, and open the main irrigation shutoff valve to flush the system and check for leaks.

■ **Hooking up near an outside faucet:** Use this method only in nonfreezing climates and then only when the line from the meter to the outside faucet is at least ¾ inch in diameter. Also the length of pipe from the water main to the manifold should be no longer than 125 feet.

Shut off the water at the meter and remove the hose bibb. Install a threaded tee and reattach the bibb. Install the main irrigation shutoff valve. Connect the main supply line and run it to the first manifold. Turn on the water at the meter, and open the main irrigation shutoff valve to flush the system and check for leaks.

■ **Hooking up near a basement meter:** Turn off the water at the valve on the street side of the water meter. Cut into the main

(Text continues on page 63)

Tying into steel pipe

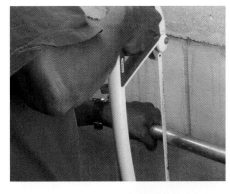

1 With water to the house shut off, cut the main service line just after the house-side stop valve. Use a hacksaw (shown) or a reciprocating saw with metal-cutting blade.

2 Using two pipe wrenches, unscrew both ends of the cut pipe. Wrap the threads of a 3- to 6-inch-long nipple with pipe-thread tape. Fasten the nipple and tee.

3 Add a short nipple to the tee. With its threads toward the joint, slip on the nut for the union. Using pipe-thread tape, attach one half of the union. Set the second half of the union in place, and measure for the length of pipe that will be added.

4 Install the length of pipe and attach the second half of the union to it. Slip the nut to the union and hand-tighten. Fully tighten the union with two wrenches.

CHANGING A GALVANIZED STEEL FITTING

When working with galvanized steel pipe, you will need a wire brush, pipe-thread tape or pipe compound, and two pipe wrenches. (If you have to extend a steel system, buy adapters to make the transition to plastic or copper—both are cheaper and easier to install.)

1 Use a small wire brush to remove any rust or dirt from the threads of the pipe. Add five or six clockwise wraps of pipe-thread tape. This seals the threads and eases the work of screwing on fittings.

2 Twist the fitting onto the pipe threads, and turn the fitting until it is hand-tight. Then use two wrenches to tighten further—one wrench to hold the pipe, and the other to tighten the fitting a few more turns. Check that the fitting faces the right direction for the next pipe. Adjust as needed by tightening—not by loosening.

Tying into copper

1 With the water shut off, cut the main service line using a tubing cutter. Don't use a hacksaw; it makes too rough a cut and can dent the pipe out of round.

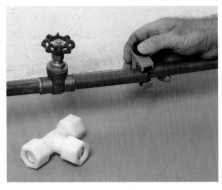

2 Remove the nuts and ferrules from the tee, hold the tee against the pipe, and mark your second cut.

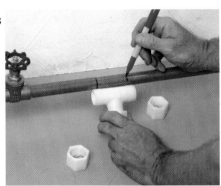

3 Complete the second cut. Slip the nuts into place, making sure their threaded ends face toward the fitting. Slip the ferrules onto the pipe, then tighten the nuts. No pipe-thread tape is needed.

SWEATING COPPER JOINTS

1 Cut the pipe using a tubing cutter, and dry-fit your assembly. Pieces should fit together snugly but easily. Next use a multiuse wire brush (shown) or other wire brush to scour the outside of the tubing and the inside of the fitting where it will be soldered.

2 Using a small flux brush, apply flux to the outside of the pipe where you cleaned it, and to the inside of the fitting. A thin, even layer on both areas is all you need. Then fit the pieces together.

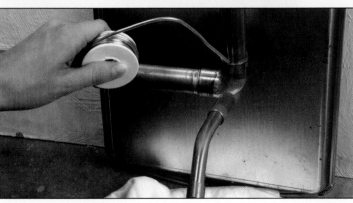

3 Use a torch to begin heating the pipe and fitting on the side closest to you. Then move the torch to the back side of the fitting. When the flux begins to smoke and run out of the joint, apply the tip of a piece of solder to the joint. It should melt quickly and flow into the connection. Use a damp rag to wipe any excess solder into the joint. Let the joint cool completely before turning on the water.

service line just after the meter and before any existing pressure regulators. Add a tee and install the main irrigation shutoff valve as in the previous procedures.

Now install another length of pipe directly after the shutoff valve and add a manual drain. The shutoff can be closed during cold weather and the cap removed to drain this part of the system.

Drill a hole through the foundation near where the backflow preventer and first manifold will be located, using a 1-inch masonry bit or a chisel. Don't make the hole any larger than necessary. Run the connecting pipe through the hole, sloping it slightly downward. Seal the wall with two-part plumber's epoxy or hydraulic cement. Turn on the water at the meter and open the main irrigation shutoff valve to flush the system and check for leaks.

▓ **Capping off:** If you can't immediately proceed with installing the line to your valve manifold, cap it off to keep the line clear of dirt and debris. With PVC you can glue a cap in place. Then when you're ready to proceed, cut it off and add an adapter to continue the line. Caps can also be friction fitted to temporarily seal off the line.

Preventing backflow

Sprinkler systems must include backflow prevention. When irrigation is suddenly turned off, siphonlike conditions can occur, sucking dirt, bacteria, fungi, pesticides, and other contaminants from around the sprinkler heads into the irrigation piping and, eventually, into your home's plumbing system. If sprinkler heads are located at a higher elevation than the manifolds, the danger is increased. Most municipal codes or water districts have specific requirements about backflow preventers, so check before you purchase.

▓ **Antisiphon valves:** Many local codes require antisiphon valves on all subsurface irrigation systems. These are basically control valves that include a backflow prevention (antisiphon) device. They are available in automatic and manual forms. Most codes require you to install an antisiphon valve 6 inches above the highest lawn sprinkler. For more information on installing antisiphon valves, see page 65.

▓ **Dedicated backflow preventers:** Some municipalities require the control valves and the backflow prevention devices be kept separate. There are three commonly used types of backflow preventers.

▼ **Backflow prevention devices are essential for protecting your home's water supply from the incursion of dirt, bacteria, pesticides, and other potential contaminants that your irrigation system might siphon in.**

BACKFLOW PREVENTERS

Vacuum breaker

Double-check backflow preventer

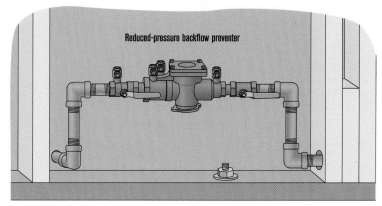
Reduced-pressure backflow preventer

Vacuum breakers are the most common backflow preventers, usually installed 12 inches above the highest lawn sprinkler head. This height difference is vital, because the devices are effective only when they are higher than the sprinkler heads. They can't be used in hilly yards where sprinkler heads are at higher elevations than the control valves. Atmospheric vacuum breakers are inexpensive, but you'll need one for each zone. Pressure-type vacuum breakers cost more, but one works for the whole system.

Another type, *double-check backflow preventers,* can be installed above or belowground and are not affected by the height of surrounding sprinklers. They are more expensive than vacuum breakers and are usually reserved for hilly terrain.

A final type, called *reduced-pressure backflow preventers,* is mandatory in some areas. One will cover the whole system, although other backflow preventers may be required as well. They must be vented and cannot be installed below the ground.

Installing valves and related components

The next step is to connect the necessary valves and install the wiring. If the water capacity of the system is greater than 80 gpm, first install a pressure regulator to control the water pressure. Install it behind the main irrigation shutoff valve, between two lengths of pipe. See page 35 to learn how to determine capacity of the system.

▓ **Main supply line:** Cut a length of pipe to run from the shutoff valve to the first manifold, then another to run from the shutoff valve to the second manifold, linking the two with a tee. The main line should be installed in trenches at the same depth as the rest of the system. Try to grade it slightly so one section is lower than the rest, and install an automatic drain valve at that point. See page 70.

▓ **Backflow device hookup:** Most irrigation systems use antisiphon valves and do not require a separate backflow device. If yours does require one, install it either between the main irrigation shutoff valve and the control valves (manifold) if it is intended to control the entire system, or after the control valve if one backflow device is needed per zone. Double-check type backflow preventers are usually installed underground in an inground valve box. Vacuum breakers are necessarily placed above ground on risers at an appropriate height (usually 12 inches higher than the highest sprinkler head in the zone). All backflow devices should be placed over a bed of 6 to 8 inches of gravel. Exact instructions for each are included with the product.

▓ **Control valve hookup:** Control valves turn each zone on and off automatically. They are generally grouped in manifolds, usually one in the front yard, one in the back. See page 66 for more on manifolds.

▓ **Installing antisiphon valves:** This installation method is the same for automatic or manual antisiphon valves. Antisiphon valves (*right*) are the most common control valves; many municipal codes require them. They must be raised above ground on risers to a height of 6 inches (or more if required by codes). Space them 5 inches apart in the manifold for easy assembly and maintenance and at least that far from the house.

To assemble a series of antisiphon valves into a manifold, turn off the main irrigation shutoff valve and assemble the

(Text continues on page 68)

PROTECTING THE SYSTEM WITH A PRESSURE-TYPE VACUUM BREAKER

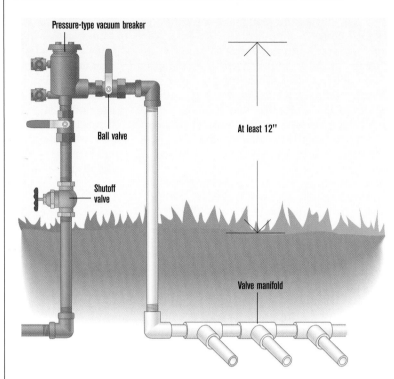

INSTALLING ANTISIPHON VALVES IN A MANIFOLD

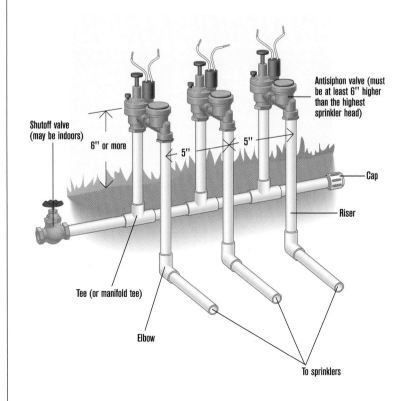

■ PVC

Solvent-welded joints cannot be taken apart. If you make a mistake, the only remedy is to cut out the affected pipe and fitting and redo the installation, adding a coupling if necessary to extend the pipe to the length needed.

1 Cut the pipe to length using plastic-pipe cutters or a fine-bladed saw. Use a deburring tool (shown) or file to remove burrs. Wipe the area to be "welded."

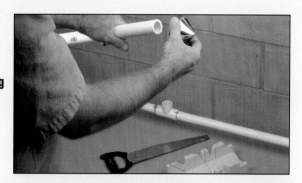

2 Apply the primer to the outside of the tubing and the inside of the fitting. Once the primer has evaporated, apply cement to each part. Quickly insert the pipe into the fitting, and give it a quarter turn to distribute the cement. Hold it in place for about 30 seconds, then wipe away any excess solvent from the joint.

3 Before turning on the water, allow the cement to set for the length of time recommended by the manufacturer. If the pipe is to be buried, wait at least 12 hours.

■ POLY

Poly uses barbed fittings with hose clamps to create a secure connection. It is much easier to install than PVC.

Warming poly pipe in the sun for an hour or so will soften the pipe and make it easier to work with. Or use a heat gun to soften the pipe.

1 Cut poly pipe evenly to the length needed with tubing shears (shown) or a hacksaw. Then slip a stainless-steel hose clamp over the pipe and insert the fitting into the end of the hose.

2 Position the clamp over the ridged section of the fitting and tighten it gently. Many new poly fittings have hose clamps built into the fittings, so you may not need to purchase separate hose clamps.

BUILDING VALVE MANIFOLDS

1 Begin by assembling a tee and a PVC nipple for each valve in the manifold. The valves need to be at least 5 inches apart.

2 Glue the open end of the nipple to the inlet of the next tee. Repeat this until you have glued together enough tees for the valves. Add an extra nipple and cap at the end of the line to ease future additions.

3 Once the basic manifold is assembled, cement another short nipple and a zone control valve to the remaining outlet on each tee.

4 Once the manifold is completed, attach it to the water supply line. Before you cement the manifold to the supply line, be sure no dirt has fallen into any openings.

5 Once all the cement has set, turn on the water and check for leaks. Then manually flush each valve using its bleed screw. Run the wiring for the valves, leaving enough extra wire to easily make connections. Finally, add a valve box and backfill with soil.

TRENCHING

Two days before digging, water hard soil moderately to soften it. Don't dig more trench than you can install pipe in one session. Trenches dug up one weekend, with pipe installation planned for the next, could become a muddy mess or even collapse if you get rain in the meantime.

Several types of digging machines are available at rental stores. Whether you plan to dig the trenches by hand or with power equipment, consider renting a sod cutter, which carefully cuts out a narrow strip of sod that you can put safely to one side.

To use pipe pullers (see photo, page 26) mark the location of the lines on the lawn with spray paint, then simply follow along them with the plow. Take care to ensure the trench is at the correct depth along its entire length. To pull PVC pipe, first glue all the pieces together and allow them to dry completely (wait at least an hour).

The rental store should provide you with detailed instructions for using a trencher (see photo, page 27). Use a trencher only through lawns, not flower beds or groundcover. It should not be operated near buildings, on steep slopes, or over any buried utility lines (check with your local gas, electric, telephone, and cable TV companies).

To dig without a pipe puller or trencher, use a straight-edged shovel and dig V-shaped trenches 6 to 12 inches deep. A depth of 12 inches is best for main lines in cold climates, but 6 inches is sufficient as long as you install drain valves. In lawn areas, first remove the sod and put it to one side, then dig the trench and place the soil you remove on the other side.

If possible plan the system so you won't have to run lines underneath sidewalks, walls, or driveways. Otherwise, to work your way under such obstacles with the least effort, try digging underneath with a crowbar or forcing a length of 1-inch metal pipe through with a hammer. For a wide obstacle, such as a sidewalk, use water power.

Attach a hose to a length of pipe with a hose adapter. The pipe must be at least 12 inches longer than the width of the slab. Dig a trench on both sides of the spot where the tunnel should be dug, making sure there is enough room to maneuver the length of pipe. Put on safety goggles and gloves and turn on the water, pushing the pipe under the sidewalk and working it back and forth as the water pressure blasts a hole. After the irrigation pipe is inserted, solidify it by pushing as much soil as possible under the slab.

DIGGING A TRENCH

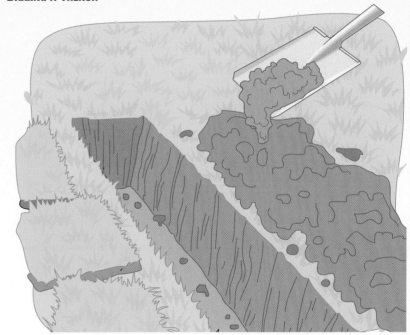

USING WATERPOWER TO DIG A TUNNEL

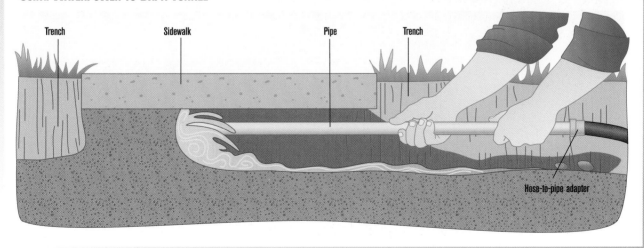

Trench   Sidewalk   Pipe   Trench

Hose-to-pipe adapter

INSTALLING THE SYSTEM *(continued)*

required number of manifold tees, 5 inches or more apart, using short sections of PVC pipe or special manifold pipe. Add a cap at the last tee of each manifold. This cap allows you to easily add more valves if needed. In freezing areas add a manual drain valve instead of a cap to facilitate drainage.

Next add an appropriate length of threaded PVC riser (remember, the antisiphon valve must be at least 6 inches higher than the highest head in the yard) to each manifold tee, then attach an antisiphon valve to each riser. Some antisiphon valves require an adapter. Add another section of riser down from the valve to the bottom of the trench, then an elbow to direct the header pipe on its planned path. Turn off the control valves and turn on the water in the entire system to check for leaks, then open the control valves to flush out any dirt.

Do not install a valve of any kind, automatic or manual, downstream from an antisiphon valve or its antisiphon function will not work.

▓ **Installing in-line or manual angle valves:** If you use an unregulated water supply such as a well or tank, or if the local code requires a separate backflow prevention device, use either automatic in-line valves or manual angle valves. They are installed in manifolds in the same manner as antisiphon valves but are usually placed underground in an inground valve box over a bed of gravel.

▓ **Wiring automatic equipment:** Use 18-gauge wire approved for underground burial to

INSTALLING AUTOMATIC IN-LINE VALVES IN A MANIFOLD

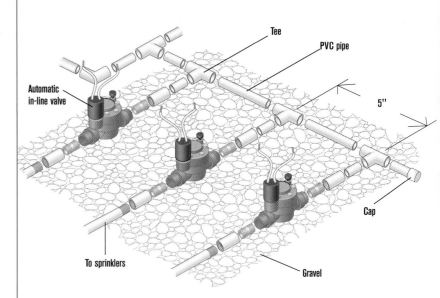

Tee
PVC pipe
5"
Automatic in-line valve
Cap
To sprinklers
Gravel

INSTALLING PIPE, ELBOWS, AND TEES

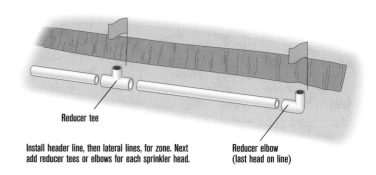

Reducer tee

Reducer elbow (last head on line)

Install header line, then lateral lines, for zone. Next add reducer tees or elbows for each sprinkler head.

Cut each riser to appropriate length

Install risers in fittings

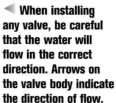

◀ **When installing any valve, be careful that the water will flow in the correct direction. Arrows on the valve body indicate the direction of flow.**

68 *SPRINKLER IRRIGATION*

attach automatic control valves to the controller. Bury the wire in trenches at least 6 inches deep. Use waterproof connectors (sometimes called "grease caps") to make connections. See page 98, for instructions for installing automatic equipment.

Laying the pipe

Up to this point you've been using PVC pipe (or metal pipe if required by local codes) to protect the system from damage due to pressure surges. After the installation of the control valves, however, using flexible poly pipe becomes feasible. See page 49 for help deciding whether to do so. To connect poly pipe to PVC, insert the end of the pipe over the ridges of a PVC-to-poly adapter and tighten a stainless-steel clamp over the pipe.

If you are using a trencher or pipe puller, dig all trenches at this stage. Otherwise, you may want to assemble each zone first, hook it up to its control valve, and test it before digging the trenches. If the soil is rocky or the trench bottom irregular, fill in with sand; moisten it and tamp it down.

Start by laying the header line from the manifold to the end of its path, then attach the lateral lines—the ones to which the sprinkler heads will actually be connected—

▶ **Flexible risers make it easy to set sprinkler heads at the right level. They are also useful for dealing with obstructions.**

TWO USES FOR FLEXIBLE RISER PIPE (SWING PIPE)

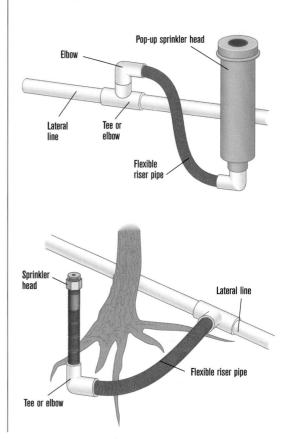

Pop-up sprinkler head

Elbow

Lateral line

Tee or elbow

Flexible riser pipe

Sprinkler head

Lateral line

Flexible riser pipe

Tee or elbow

INSTALLATION ON SLOPES

There are two rules for installing sprinklers on slopes. First, because sprinkler heads will not water in a perfect circle (gravity will cause the throw radius in the lower sector to lengthen and that in the upper sector to shorten), you must place the heads closer to the uphill side of the slope to maintain a proper spacing pattern. Second, always align sprinkler heads perpendicular to the slope, to prevent erosion on the uphill side.

PROPER PLACING OF HEADS ON SLOPES

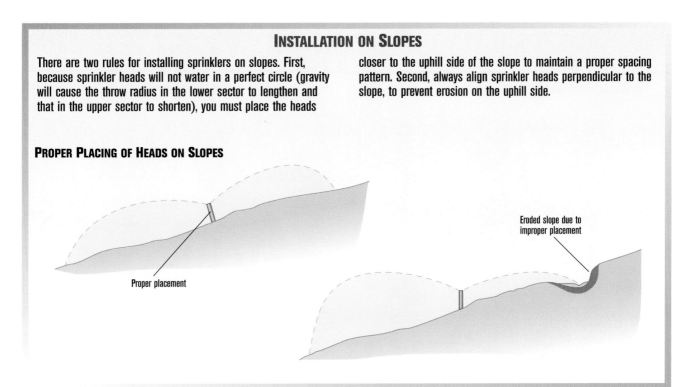

Proper placement

Eroded slope due to improper placement

► **After the spray heads are installed, adjust the pattern and rate of flow.**

to the header line. Lay the piping at the correct depth. At the base of each automatic drain valve or self-draining header, remove 6 inches of sand and soil and replace it with gravel; pack it down well. Repeat with the next zone. Make all connections with appropriate elbows and tees.

Attaching risers and sprinkler heads

Insert a reducer tee for each sprinkler head (substitute a reducer elbow for the last head on each line). Next add a riser to each tee. Adjustable risers, although more expensive, are a good choice, as soil builds up in lawns and gardens over time and, when this happens, the risers can simply be twisted slightly to extend their length. Use a flexible riser or swing joint in zones of

AUTOMATIC DRAIN VALVES

Where temperatures drop below freezing, you must install automatic drain valves at the lowest point in each zone. Drain valves are small threaded devices designed to remain shut when the water is under pressure and open when the water is turned off. They are easily attached to any underground line by means of a combination tee inserted in the pipe. They should be turned downward from the line to allow for proper drainage. If you prefer, a short length of pipe can be slipped over the drain valve to keep it from blocking. Add at least one automatic drain valve per line, inserting it at the lowest point, so that no water remains standing in the pipes between waterings. This is essential in cold climates to prevent the pipes from cracking and is valuable elsewhere as well.

In some cases you might prefer to use a self-draining header rather than a drain valve. Many models of pop-up impact sprinklers, for example, have two inlets, one on the side for water connection and one on the bottom for an automatic drain valve, allowing it to drain after each use. The bottom inlet can be plugged in warm climates, but a drain valve should be installed in each one in freezing climates. Place all automatic drain valves and self-draining headers over a small bed of gravel into which excess water can drain.

INSTALLING AUTOMATIC DRAIN VALVES

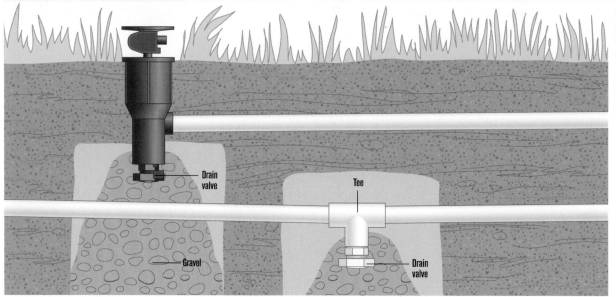

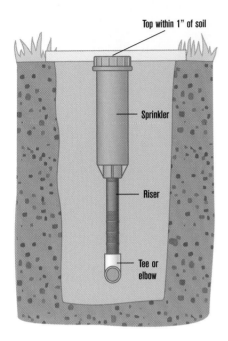

Top within 1" of soil

Sprinkler

Riser

Tee or elbow

heavy traffic. Make sure each riser is vertical (except on slopes), and cut it to the appropriate height using a hacksaw. Stationary and pop-up lawn sprinkler heads should be within 1 inch of the soil, allowing room for the grass to grow and establish itself. Mount shrub heads as high as the expected maximum height of the plantings in that sector.

A depth of 6 inches is usually sufficient for sprinkler trenches, but extra-high pop-up heads might require greater depth. Seal each riser, except the one at the end of the zone, with a pipe plug and flush the system until the water runs clean. Next turn off the water, remove the plugs from each riser, and flush again. Turn off the water when finished.

Install the appropriate sprinkler on each riser. Applying pipe joint tape around the riser head will offer extra protection against leaks. Tie the riser to the stake or flag to keep it vertical.

Checking and adjusting the zone

Turn off any water running in the house and turn on the water in the zone being installed. Check for leaks, then adjust for proper coverage. Starting with the sprinkler closest to the control valve, adjust its flow with a screwdriver (some rotary heads have a flap to adjust). Next redirect any part-circle spray patterns as needed. Impact heads have friction collars at the base of the nozzle for this purpose. A special key or ratchet (supplied by the manufacturer) is often needed to adjust the pattern of rotary heads. Repeat for each head. If there are spots not being properly watered, make adjustments. This may involve using different heads, respacing heads, adding heads, or moving a head from one zone to another.

Finishing the job

At day's end and after PVC pipe has set for at least 12 hours, fill in the trenches. First cover the pipes with a layer of sand, then backfill with soil. Allow the soil to settle before resodding the area. Tamp the soil or flood the trench to speed settling, add more soil to bring the trench up to level, then carefully tamp sod in place. You are now ready to water one entire sector with your new irrigation system.

▼ **Watch to ensure that shrub, ground cover, and other plant foliage doesn't distort the spray, then adjust sprinkler heads as needed.**

MICRO-IRRIGATION

Microirrigation has long been considered the wave of the future. In fact, the future is already here. Microirrigation is now widely used in home watering systems of all kinds. Irrigation specialists include microirrigation in their projects as a matter of course, either in combination with sprinkler irrigation or on its own, and so can you. Setting up microirrigation can be as simple as running a porous hose through the garden and turning on the water, or it can involve the same precise planning, trenching, and piping necessary for a sprinkler system.

This chapter presents the different possibilities so you can decide whether microirrigation is appropriate for your garden and, if so, what kind. You will also discover several different ways of installing microirrigation, ranging from the simple to the complex.

▼ **Low-pressure, low-volume microirrigation distributes water without waste. Here, micro-sprinklers located in the pergola overhead provide a fine mist that cools the air and raises humidity around orchids and ferns growing in hanging baskets.**

How microsystems work

Drip and microirrigation systems use a special pressure reducer/filter to maintain a consistent, lower water pressure. This allows the system to apply water slowly over longer periods of time. Traditional drip irrigation uses drip emitters, which apply water drop by drop directly to the ground at the base of plants. Because there is no water spray, the problem of evaporation loss is nearly eliminated.

Microirrigation uses miniature sprayers to water more like a sprinkler, but it applies water slowly to small areas.

Both systems are designed to keep the root zone soil consistently moist (see page 74). As a result, drip and microirrigation systems reduce plant stress and promote solid, healthy growth.

THE BASICS OF MICROIRRIGATION

Microirrigation is an increasingly popular choice in landscaping. It is inexpensive, easy to install, and adaptable to many uses. It may be just the system you need.

Precision watering

If this book had been written a few years ago, this chapter would have been called "Drip Irrigation," because nearly all low-pressure irrigation systems watered plants drop by drop. Today low-pressure irrigation systems spray and mist as well as drip, so microirrigation is a more appropriate term. Some professionals still use "drip irrigation" to refer to all forms of microirrigation.

Although sprinkler and microirrigation systems seem to have much in common, they are actually quite different. Sprinklers deliver a lot of water quickly and are designed for a drench-and-let-dry cycle. Sometimes much of the water drains away unused because it was applied too quickly for the soil and the plants to absorb.

Microirrigation, on the other hand, keeps the root zone evenly moist at all times yet never so wet that the plants become waterlogged and subject to rot. It delivers small amounts of water more often and over a longer period of time. Microirrigation emitters typically supply ½ to 2 gallons of water per hour (gph)—quite a contrast with sprinklers, whose flow is calculated in gallons per minute. No effort is made to soak the entire area from above. When applied slowly, water spreads laterally underground. You simply place emitters close enough together that their coverage zones meet.

Given its low flow rate, microirrigation doesn't require high water pressure. In fact, most systems must operate under low pressure. That's good news if the local system suffers bouts of low pressure, but most people will have to reduce the pressure coming from their supply line. This can be done by installing a pressure reducer at the beginning of the system, by using pressure-compensating emitters, or by combining the two.

Recent developments

Clogged emitters were once a serious concern because so little water flowed from their narrow openings that they were next to impossible to flush. Most modern emitters, however, use a turbulent-flow design that keeps dirt particles in continuous motion and prevents them from settling inside the emitter. Modern emitters also reduce the speed of flow, allowing water to flow drop by drop from a larger opening that is less subject to clogging. Even with these new emitters, however, you must take care to include all of the required filters specified for a system and to periodically flush and clean them as recommended by the manufacturer.

ZONES OF IRRIGATION JOINED UNDERGROUND

Moist soil

◀ A drip emitter hose has emitters preinstalled in the hose. It works well for areas with evenly spaced rows, such as vegetable gardens.

Newer emitters solve another problem: Older ones exposed to the sun's ultraviolet rays eventually became brittle and broke. Newer plastics don't have that limitation; they stand up well to long use.

One problem with the new emitters remains: Many are small and project from the ground, leaving them susceptible to damage from foot traffic. The aboveground parts of microirrigation systems require the same careful placement as those of sprinkler components, and they must never be installed in lawns or where a lawn mower might hit them. See page 43 for more information on placement.

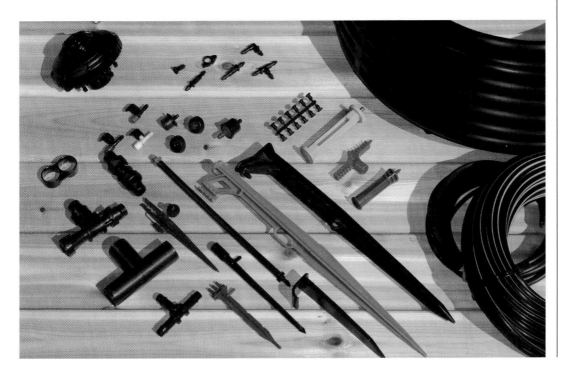

◀ The array of products for microirrigation is greater than for sprinkler systems.

SELECTING COMPONENTS

▶ **Piping includes ½-inch poly pipe and ¼-inch vinyl tubing.**

Microirrigation offers an even wider variety of components than does sprinkler irrigation. Here are the elements you need to look at before you begin to plan a microirrigation system.

Choosing the whole ensemble

The choices in microirrigation are bewildering. Each company supplies a full range of drip emitters, sprinklers, misters, porous pipe, and in-line emitters, not to mention pipes, stakes, and fittings. Often these parts, though they look alike, are not readily interchangeable. For example, most irrigation parts are now color-coded to make replacing them easier; however different manufacturers don't necessarily use the same color codes. Purchase all components from the same manufacturer.

Pipes

The choice is easy here: Microirrigation systems all use ½-inch polyethylene landscape pipe for at least the supply and header lines and sometimes all the lines. One-quarter-inch or, more rarely, ⅛-inch vinyl tubing (sometimes called spaghetti tubing) serves for lead-in tubes and lateral lines, especially for container gardens and microsprinkler systems. To connect the supply line to the water system, elementary aboveground drip systems often use garden hose, but more permanent situations

▼ **Porous pipe emits water from numerous tiny pores spaced along its entire surface.**

generally call for buried PVC or poly pipe for the main line.

Emitters

There are four categories of emitters: porous pipe, punch-in emitters, emitter lines, and microsprinkler heads.

▪ **Porous pipe:** Porous pipe is the easiest and least expensive irrigation option. Snake it around plantings, hook it up to an existing hose, and turn it on. Hide it with a bit of mulch. Usually made of recycled tires, it oozes water from tiny pores. How far the water travels horizontally varies according to your conditions, so do some tests before deciding on the permanent location of the pipe. Of course the location doesn't have to be permanent. Simply pick up porous pipe and move it as needed. It can also be buried 2 to 6 inches deep and become part of a permanent system. Porous pipe can be cut into sections and placed in lateral lines to give coverage similar to that of poly pipe.

On the negative side, due to the numerous pores situated irregularly over the entire surface, inner water pressure control is not possible. As a result porous pipe waters unevenly, losing pressure toward the end of each length and overwatering low parts of its run while letting higher ones dry out. It can therefore be used efficiently only on flat ground. It is especially important to use a fine filter (about 200 mesh), because the pores are easily clogged. The fittings for porous pipe tend to come apart under even moderate pressure, so use a special pressure regulator to keep the zone below 10 psi at all times.

Porous pipe is most often used in flower beds and vegetable gardens, under hedges, around large trees, and in mass plantings of shrubs—areas where its slightly uneven water delivery will not cause problems.

◀ **Mini rotating sprinklers have a 10-foot maximum spray radius.**

■ **Punch-in emitters:** These water outlets can be inserted directly into pipe after you punch a hole into it. They have an inlet barb at their base so that they won't pop back out. They can be installed anywhere along ½-inch poly pipe; simply make a hole with a hole punch and put one in. Or they can be inserted in the end sections of ¼-inch or ⅛-inch tubing. Some emitters have self-piercing inlet barbs to punch their own holes. Just push and twist, and they're in.

Emitters come in regular and pressure-compensating forms. The latter are the better choice. They give off the same amount of water throughout the zone, even when there is a major difference in elevation or the tubing is particularly long.

Punch-in emitters have different flow rates, usually ½, 1, 2, and sometimes 4 gallons per hour. In general, use ½-gph emitters for clay soils, 1-gph emitters for loam soils, and 2-gph emitters for sandy soils. If you are unsure of your soil type, use 1-gph emitters. If you can see that some emitters in your system are not supplying enough water, simply replace them with those that are one flow rate higher, or add more emitters. If some sectors get too much water, replace the emitters with those of a lower flow rate, or remove one or two emitters and plug the resulting holes.

The three main types of punch-in emitters are drip emitters, misters, and in-line drip emitters.

Drip emitters: The most popular punch-in emitters, these are suitable for containers, vegetable gardens, flower gardens, trees, and shrubs. They make up the foundation of drip irrigation, literally delivering water drop by drop and keeping the surface of the soil almost dry while keeping roots moist. They can be punched into ½-inch pipe laid on the ground or inserted into the ends of ¼-inch or ⅛-inch tubing and held off the ground by stakes. Some manufacturers produce drip emitters incorporated into stakes.

▼ **Secure emitters at a desired height and location.**

Misters: These are most popular in greenhouses and with specialists who grow high-humidity plants such as ferns and bromeliads. Otherwise they are used in very dry climates to keep fine-leaved annuals, perennials, and tropicals in top shape and to add cooling mist to patio areas. In less arid climates, gardeners sometimes use them to humidify hanging baskets. Most give off a fine mist that humidifies the air but rarely collects on the leaves. Those designed to give larger water droplets serve a double purpose: They moisten the air, and the droplets that form drip down to the base of the plant to water its roots. Because misters must be run at regular intervals during the day, but only for a few minutes at a time, they should be on a different zone than any other emitter and preferably on a timer.

When using misters, attach them to their pot using a clip or stake; each manufacturer has its own device. Some misters come incorporated into a special combination stake that inserts into potting soil or is nailed or screwed to an outside support.

▲ **Misters attached to risers gently apply water to plants that benefit from top-down watering.**

In-line drip emitters: These emitters are a hybrid between a drip emitter and an emitter line. Like punch-in emitters, they are inserted individually into the water line according to need. Like emitter lines, however, they fit right into the line and not on its periphery. Water simply flows through them and continues on, allowing some water to drip out as it passes. In-line emitters are simple to install. Cut the tubing wherever water is needed, insert the barbed ends into the cut section of the tube, and push back together. Most are designed for ¼-inch tubing only. They have a more limited range of flow rates than do drip emitters, usually only ½ or 1 gph. In-line emitters are used mostly in flower boxes and vegetable gardens because they are most efficient at watering small plants in short rows.

■ **Emitter lines:** Emitter lines incorporate equally spaced emitters directly into ½-inch pipe. As water runs through the line, some drips out. The emitters come preinstalled at 12-, 18-, 24-, and 36-inch spacings and are rated to dispense ½, 1, or 2 gph of water. Lines with ½-gph emitters are used for clay soils, lines with 1-gph emitters for loam soils, and lines with 2-gph emitters for sandy soils.

All emitter lines have the turbulent-flow design to keep them from clogging. In most cases, especially on a long line or on a steep slope, use pressure-compensating emitter lines.

Sold in rolls, emitter lines can be cut to length and connected to the main line or other laterals in the same way as any other poly pipe. These practical and durable watering devices give excellent results in

TWO TYPES OF IN-LINE EMITTERS

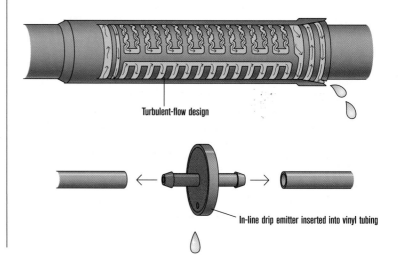

Turbulent-flow design

In-line drip emitter inserted into vinyl tubing

flower beds and vegetable gardens, under hedges, around large trees, and in mass plantings of shrubs. They are simply laid on the ground and covered with mulch. They are also much less subject to breakage than punch-in emitters because the emitters are actually part of the pipe and can't accidentally be pulled apart. On the down side, the regularly spaced emitters don't allow as much flexibility as individual emitters do. Emitter lines are most practical where groupings of similar plants are evenly spaced.

■ **Microsprinkler heads:** Microsprinkler heads take their place between sprinkler irrigation and microirrigation, right where the differences begin to dissolve. These heads are also sometimes called low-volume sprayers. These microsprinklers are the main reason why "drip irrigation" is no longer an entirely appropriate term to describe low-volume irrigation systems. Microsprinkler heads use low water pressure and narrow-diameter pipes as drip systems do, yet apply water in a fanlike spray as sprinklers do. They are not as efficient as punch-in and in-line microirrigation, because they lose some water through evaporation, yet they waste less water than high-pressure sprinklers.

You can think of microsprinkler heads as less powerful relatives of high-pressure heads. They can spray in full circles or increments of a circle, even in strips. Most cover a radius of 6 to 11 feet and are ideal for small beds. They are usually set in beds on tubelike risers and don't retract into the ground after use. With careful placement they are relatively inconspicuous because they are so narrow. These heads are most popular in flower beds, mass plantings of shrubs and perennials, and groundcovers. Because they don't retract and have restricted range, they can't be used on lawns other than as incidental sprayers in areas of overlap.

Microbubblers are based on the same principle as microsprinkler heads. They are used primarily for shrub plantings but also work in flower beds and groundcovers.

CONVERTING TO MICROIRRIGATION

If you already have a sprinkler system, it is often possible to convert everything but lawn areas to microirrigation without digging or removing pipes—just buy a converter or retrofit kit. These kits allow you to convert a single spray head to single or multiple microirrigation watering devices.

However, entire zones must be converted. It is not possible to have a zone that contains both high-pressure sprinklers and low-pressure microirrigation.

First, turn off the water at the main sprinkler shutoff valve and twist off the old sprinkler head to reveal the riser. Turn on the zone to flush out any sediment. Install on the riser the appropriate adapter for the kind of converter kit you have chosen, plus the converter itself. Single-outlet emission devices permit you to convert one sprinkler head to a single microirrigation device. Multioutlet emission devices allow you to add, for each original sprinkler head, six or more outlets that each can have lengths of ¼-inch poly tubing added to direct the drip-irrigation flow in any direction. If all outlets

are not needed immediately (as is often the case), don't remove the plugs from the unneeded ones; keep them for future use. For exact installation details follow the manufacturer's instructions.

In the case of pop-up sprinklers where the riser is underground beneath the housing and hard to reach, it is often easier to use the housing as an adapter than to remove it. Many suppliers offer a retrofit kit designed for this purpose. These kits are not universal, however. Make sure that the kit you choose is adapted to the sprinkler line. To install, remove the nozzle mechanism of the pop-up sprinkler from the housing and insert the retrofit kit: a pressure regulator, filter, and section of threaded riser. Attach the microirrigation device of your choice to the top of the riser.

The conversion process will leave you with a number of unused spray heads that must be capped. To do so, add a ½-inch threaded cap to each unused riser. Special caps are also available to cover unused pop-up sprinkler housings.

SIZING THE MICROIRRIGATION SYSTEM

MICROIRRIGATION PLAN

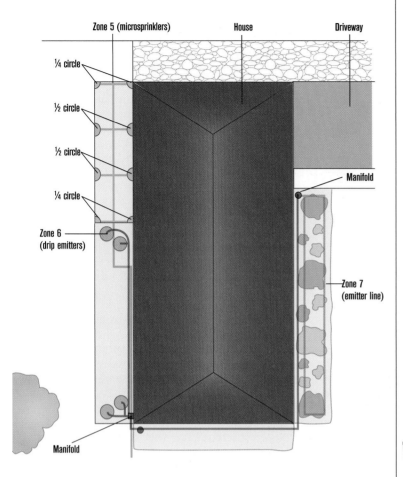

Zone 5 (microsprinklers)   House   Driveway

¼ circle

½ circle

½ circle

¼ circle

Zone 6
(drip emitters)

Manifold

Zone 7
(emitter line)

Manifold

Drawing a plot map *(above)* for microirrigation is similar to doing a sprinkler system plan (see page 50.) Just add the required microirrigation zones to the plan you have drawn of your property. Keep the manufacturer's equipment chart handy.

Microsprinkler heads can be plotted in the same way as high-pressure sprinkler heads are; you just draw smaller circles of coverage. For all other low-pressure emitter devices, just plot the lines.

Plotting mass plantings

Microirrigation pipe is generally laid out as a series of relatively parallel lateral lines that eventually form a rectangular shape. Using parallel lines set 12 to 24 inches apart (that is, at distances where two water spreads meet) is the most efficient way to ensure even watering. Set the lines closer (12 inches) in sandy soils, farther apart (18 to 24 inches) in loam or clay soils.

Connect parallel lateral lines to a single ½-inch supply line, called the header line, which connects back to the main supply line. Do not add emitters to the header or main supply lines. Connect the supply and lateral lines using tees and elbows.

The end of each lateral line must be closed off. This is done with an end closure (see page 88). Each line can terminate with its own end closure, or you can close the rectangle by adding another piece of supply line that leads to a single end closure per zone (see facing page). The latter option takes more effort to install, but is less work in the long run because microirrigation lines must be drained periodically, and it is easier to remove two or three end closures than several dozen.

For areas watered by parallel lateral lines, you can use punch-in emitters and emitter lines interchangeably. Porous pipe can be substituted as long as you take into account its slightly irregular water delivery. Some manufacturers suggest ¼-inch vinyl tubing with in-line drip emitters for areas where short lateral lines are needed, but such tubing is more delicate to work with than standard ½-inch poly pipe and is best restricted to hanging baskets and containers where thicker pipe is undesirable.

Plotting isolated plantings

It is inefficient to water isolated plants or ones spaced at great distances, such as trees, using parallel line irrigation—you'd have more pipe than emitters. Instead run a single ½-inch supply line to within the drip line of the plant. If there are several well-spaced plants in the vicinity, snake the supply line toward each, or use tee connectors to attach additional lateral lines. There is no need to use straight lines because poly pipe is flexible.

Isolated plants will absorb water from anywhere within their root area, but, for

NUMBER OF EMITTERS PER PLANT BASED ON CANOPY DIAMETER	
Plant Canopy Diameter	**Emitters per Plant**
Up to 3'	1
3'–5'	2
6'–9'	3
10' and more	1 per 2½' of canopy diameter

PARALLEL DRIP LINES WITH TWO TYPES OF END CLOSURE

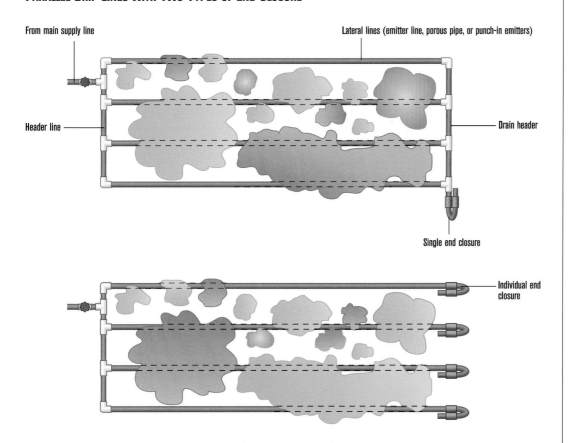

From main supply line

Lateral lines (emitter line, porous pipe, or punch-in emitters)

Header line

Drain header

Single end closure

Individual end closure

more efficient results, place emitters or an emitter line a few inches from the base of smaller plants and at about one-third to one-half the distance away from the center of the foliage canopy for larger plants. The chart *opposite* will help you determine the number of emitters needed. Watch the plant over time and adjust the number or size of emitters as needed.

For example, a small shrub needs only one emitter, but a tree with a 15-foot canopy requires six (15 divided by 2½). Use the chart on page 87 to determine the flow rate of the emitters required.

There are several ways to water a plant once the pipe has reached it.

▓ Punch emitters directly into the line.

▓ Use a short section of line as a feeder line leading from the supply line to within the plant's canopy, and add emitters. Use either ½-inch poly pipe or ¼-inch vinyl.

▓ For plants where four or more emitters will be needed, loop a short section of line around the plant and attach it to the supply line with a tee connector (see page 82). This setup is called a pigtail. You can use emitter line, porous pipe, or plain ½-inch poly pipe and emitters.

After placing the pipe, flush it. Then plug the end of the supply line and any laterals.

In many cases, you'll want to bury the supply line. If so, check municipal regulations, particularly any concerning backflow prevention. Do not bury emitters or emitter line; you may cover them with mulch instead.

IRRIGATING ISOLATED PLANTINGS

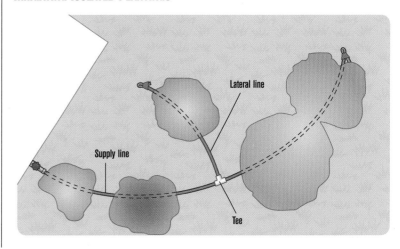

Lateral line

Supply line

Tee

Three Emitter Setups

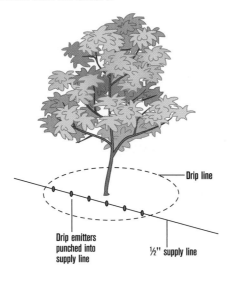

Drip line

Drip emitters punched into supply line

½" supply line

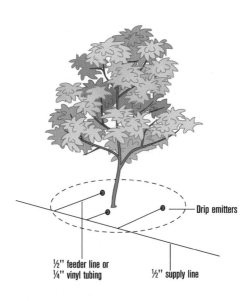

Drip emitters

½" feeder line or ¼" vinyl tubing

½" supply line

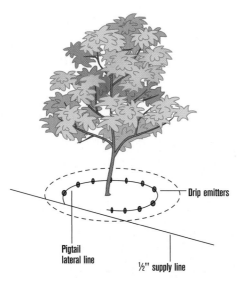

Drip emitters

Pigtail lateral line

½" supply line

Dividing into zones

Divide the system into zones according to the needs of the plants. This is easier than with sprinkler irrigation because you can adjust for localized watering needs by adding or removing emitters or changing their sizes. You can easily combine shrubs, trees, groundcovers, and flower beds on the same zone. The main determining factors for dividing microirrigation into zones are maximum line length and number of emitters required.

Almost all emitters are now pressure-compensating, meaning that zones of higher or lower elevation will receive equal amounts of water and can be combined. This, plus the fact that you can use enormously long pipe (each line can hold hundreds of emitters), means you can often group all the inground ornamental plants of a small to medium yard in one zone. Vegetable beds should, however, be on a separate zone due to their more seasonal use, as should container plants, which often require daily watering. Misters should also be on a separate zone.

■ **Line length:** The basic guideline for plain poly pipe or porous pipe is to use no more than 200 feet in a single zone.

The length of pressure-compensating emitter line per zone varies considerably depending on the spacing of the emitters and their flow rate, but it can range from 326 feet for ½-gph emitter line on 12-inch centers to 248 feet for 1-gph emitter line on 12-inch centers. As the spacing increases, so does the length of emitter line that can be used. For emitter line on 24-inch centers, the usable length per zone jumps to 584 feet for ½-gph emitter line and 444 feet for 1-gph emitter line. These numbers may vary. Consult the manufacturer's product recommendations. Use much shorter lengths of ¼-inch vinyl tubing.

■ **Number of emitters:** Like line length, the total gallonage per zone is limited; it should not be more than 150 gph. Therefore, you need to total up the gph of the emitters for each proposed zone to make sure they fall within the accepted maximum. There is plenty of leeway. You could use up to 300 ½-gph emitters (300 × ½), 150 1-gph emitters (150 × 1), or 75 2-gph emitters (75 × 2) per zone.

Microsprinklers are an exception. Their water use resembles that of sprinklers more than that of other emitters. They must always be on a separate zone from other microirrigation devices because of their

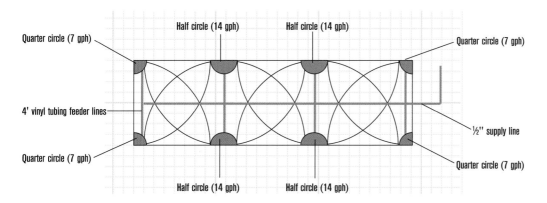

Quarter circle (7 gph)

Half circle (14 gph)

Half circle (14 gph)

Quarter circle (7 gph)

4' vinyl tubing feeder lines

½'' supply line

Quarter circle (7 gph)

Quarter circle (7 gph)

Half circle (14 gph)

Half circle (14 gph)

greater water use. The flow rate of a microsprinkler varies from 7 to 25 gph, compared to only ½ to 2 gph for most emitters. Therefore, you cannot use as many microsprinklers per zone as emitters; you probably will have to divide large microsprinkler zones into more than one zone. Take these factors into account:

▓ The radius of a microsprinkler, like that of a high-pressure sprinkler, should always overlap its neighbor's. Since there is little wind drift, the minimum overlap is only 25 percent of the diameter.

▓ Many microsprinklers require a minimum water pressure of 20 or 25 psi.

▓ Don't use more than 150 feet of ½-inch poly pipe per zone.

▓ The gallonage per zone shouldn't exceed 200 gph.

▓ Use no more than 5 feet of ¼-inch vinyl tubing between the ½-inch supply pipe and a full-circle sprinkler, or 10 feet for half-circle, quarter-circle, or strip sprinklers.

Microsprinklers vary in flow rates, so always check the manufacturer's listed specifications. For example one manufacturer rates its full-circle microsprinklers at 25 gph, its half circles at 14 gph, and its quarter circles at 7 gph. One possible zone that would remain under the 200 gph limit would be four quarter-circle microsprinklers, five half circles, and four full circles: $(4 \times 7) + (5 \times 14) + (4 \times 25) = 198$ gph.

◀ **Drip manifolds let you run emitter lines to separate plants and control the water flow to each. They are easily hidden by foliage or mulch and can be run off a spigot or a supply line. This unit has a pressure regulator and filter integrated into the manifold.**

INSTALLING MICROIRRIGATION

I f you are looking for a quick, easy, and inexpensive watering system and don't mind a few pipes in the landscape, follow the recommendations for surface installation, at *right*. If you want the system to be as permanent and integrated into the landscape as most sprinkler systems are, see the description for subsurface supply-line installation on page 86. You can also combine the two, putting parts such as supply lines underground, and others, such as lateral lines, aboveground.

LOCATING SHUTOFF VALVES

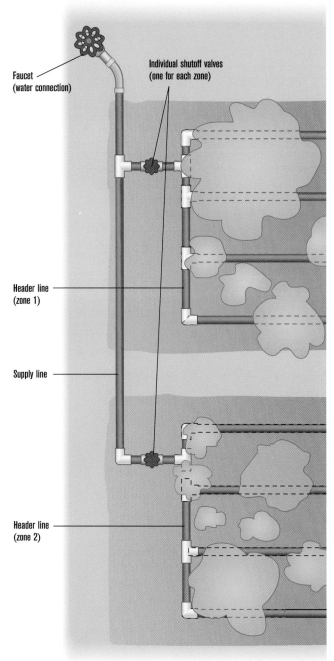

Faucet
(water connection)

Individual shutoff valves
(one for each zone)

Header line
(zone 1)

Supply line

Header line
(zone 2)

Surface installation

Surface installation does not require trenching and is so simple you can have an entire zone up and running in one afternoon. By not burying the pipe, you avoid many of the usual municipal-code restrictions on the location of a system and materials. On the other hand, it is important to plan carefully so the exposed pipe is not too visible and runs through areas where there is no foot traffic. Often this means you'll be running pipe in at least two sections: one line around the house to water foundation plantings and other nearby beds, and another line around the periphery of the lot to reach trees and shrubs planted there.

Because surface installations are often manual and connected to faucets, that type of hookup is discussed here. However, you can make a surface system automatic or hook it up as you would a subsurface installation (see page 86).

■ **Connecting to a faucet:** A proper faucet connection uses a series of connected valves that, in concert, control the system's water pressure, filtering, and backflow prevention. If there are several outdoor faucets, it might be possible for each to supply one or two zones that are turned off and on at the faucet. Usually, though, a single supply line is installed that leads from the water connection. Individual zones are then turned on and off by shutoff valves located at the head of each zone. This reduces the octopuslike assembly of pipes running from a single faucet.

Start with a dual shutoff Y-connector, with one outlet attached to the water connection and the other outlet left available. This is especially wise if the yard has only one outdoor faucet. If a second outdoor faucet is available, you could reserve it entirely for irrigation. Use the Y-connector to assemble a second water connector for another part of the irrigation system, forming a simple two-zone manifold.

Next you'll need a backflow preventer. This is essential even if your municipal code does not mention it. For surface irrigation systems, a simple faucet-type antisiphon vacuum breaker is sufficient unless the local code states otherwise. For a more detailed discussion on preventing backflow, see page 63.

The filter is next in line. Some so-called complete microirrigation kits don't include one, but a filter is essential because the emitter outlets are so narrow that even the modern turbulent-flow emitters can be clogged by a few flakes of rust or other debris. Y-filters are the best choice, since they are both efficient and easy to clean. If you're on a well system that might pick up sand, look for a sand-type Y-filter. You can also use T-filters.

The pressure regulator comes next. Although some manufacturers of pressure-compensating emitters and emitter lines claim their microirrigation products can run at normal water pressure, it would be unfortunate to see the system blow apart if the pressure rose to abnormal levels. A pressure regulator will prevent that and also prolong the life of pipes and emitters by ensuring constant low pressure. The simplest pressure-regulation device is the pressure-compensating flow control, which looks like a tiny washer. Better known and more efficient are preset pressure regulators.

Buy one appropriate to the needs of the emitters you'll be using: 15, 20, 25, and 30 psi are the most common. Be sure to install pressure regulators in the right direction; most casings have a stamped arrow indicating the direction of flow. Point the arrow in the direction of the irrigation system, not the house.

Because all the elements of the water connection are designed for ¾-inch or 1-inch connections, finish with an adapter called a line connection, into which you can insert ½-inch solid supply pipe.

As you assemble the elements of a water connection, add pipe thread tape or pipe compound to each threaded fitting to ensure a good seal. You may also need one or two hose-to-thread adapters. (Iron pipe threads are more closely spaced than hose threads are, so trying to twist one onto the other could ruin both.) You might also encounter instances in which two devices meant to fit together in the series both have either male or female threads. If so, use an adapter.

Finish the connection by bracing it, if necessary, with metal or wooden stakes, and placing a 4- to 6-inch layer of gravel under its base to help absorb water resulting from flushing the filter.

■ **Installing supply lines:** Stake out the yard according to the plan, then lay out the main supply line from the water connection to the head of each zone.

TYPICAL FAUCET CONNECTION ASSEMBLY

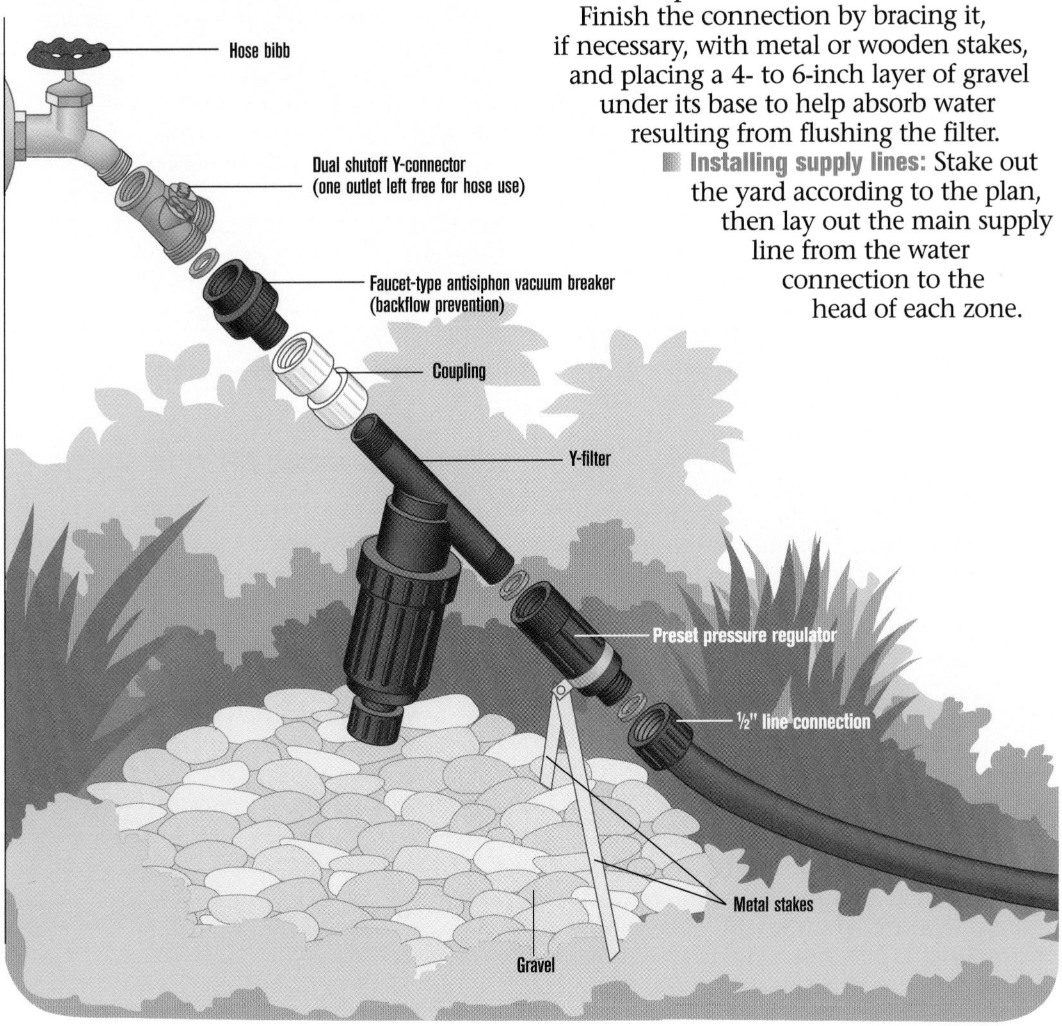

Hose bibb

Dual shutoff Y-connector (one outlet left free for hose use)

Faucet-type antisiphon vacuum breaker (backflow prevention)

Coupling

Y-filter

Preset pressure regulator

½" line connection

Metal stakes

Gravel

Compression Fittings

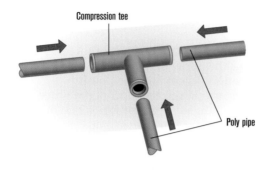

Compression tee

Poly pipe

Installing Lateral Lines

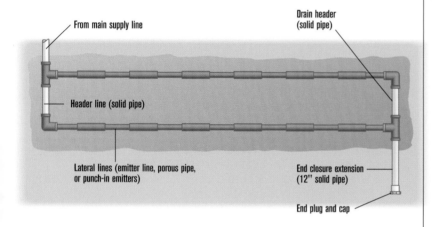

From main supply line

Drain header (solid pipe)

Header line (solid pipe)

Lateral lines (emitter line, porous pipe, or punch-in emitters)

End closure extension (12" solid pipe)

End plug and cap

The line will be less stiff and easier to manage if you let it sit in the sun first, but you'll still probably need to hold it in place with a few wire stakes. Never stretch exposed poly pipe so it is completely taut. Leave room for expansion and contraction, especially in cold climates.

Poly pipe can be assembled using couplings, tees, or elbows. Unlike ¾-inch or larger pipe, ½-inch poly pipe often uses compression fittings instead of ridged insert fittings with clamps. With insert fittings, the fitting is inserted into the pipe; with compression fittings, the pipe is inserted into the fitting. Simply push and twist until the pipe is inserted about 1 inch into the fitting; soak the end of the pipe in warm water first if it is too stiff. The fitting will cling to the poly pipe by compression, forming a perfect seal.

Begin assembling the supply lines. To link sections of pipe together, or at points where the main supply line branches or abruptly turns a corner, add a tee, elbow, or coupling. When you come to the head of a new zone, add a manual shutoff valve (a ball valve, for example). This allows you

to turn each zone on and off separately. The shutoff valves should not be inserted into the main supply line itself unless it is the last zone on the line; instead, insert the valves into a secondary section of supply line, because each zone must be turned on and off independently from the others.

From the shutoff valve, add supply line as needed to reach the spot where the header line will be placed. Now turn on the water and flush. You are ready to install the zone. See page 88 for detailed information on lateral-line installation.

Subsurface supply-line installation

This is the best option for an inconspicuous system because all supply pipe is safely underground. Subsurface irrigation systems will last longer and should be considered the only truly permanent microirrigation system. On the other hand, burying pipe means you'll have to investigate local codes, do a great deal of trenching, and spend longer doing the installation.

The installation of subsurface supply lines is similar to that described for sprinkler systems in the previous chapter. You have the same decisions to make in determining which valves you need, grouping them in manifolds, staking, and trenching. Microirrigation systems can share the same manifolds as sprinkler systems and the same controllers, as long as they are on separate zones and have a pressure regulator. Although the two may

Bringing Underground Pipe to the Surface

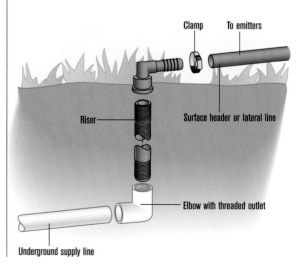

Clamp

To emitters

Riser

Surface header or lateral line

Elbow with threaded outlet

Underground supply line

be watering different sectors of the yard at different pressures, they are all part of the same system. As with sprinkler systems, either poly or PVC pipe can be used from the water connection to the head of the zone.

Although a pressure regulator is not used in most sprinkler systems, it is essential to microirrigation. Its purpose and installation are described in the section on connecting to a faucet on page 84. It should be placed as the last element of the manifold, at a rate of one regulator per zone.

Emitters are usually set aboveground, even in subsurface microirrigation. Only porous hose and treated emitter line are ever fully buried. Subsurface supply lines are set 8 to 12 inches deep. This means the supply line will have to be brought to the surface level again to join the header. To do this, use an elbow joint and a piece of PVC pipe or poly pipe acting as a riser.

With subsurface installation, 1-inch or ¾-inch PVC or poly pipe is commonly used for all underground sections up to the header lines, which are usually made

of ½-inch poly pipe (sometimes PVC pipe). Use a reducing fitting to join the two sections. Finish by flushing the installation well.

DRIP-EMITTER PLACEMENT

Soil Type	Emitter Flow	Plant Spacing	Preferred Emitter Placement
Clay	½ gph	Up to 24"	Every 24"
		25" or more	1 per plant*
Loam	1 gph	Up to 18"	Every 18"
		19" or more	1 per plant*
Sand	2 gph	Up to 12"	Every 12"
		3" or more	1 per plant*

*For small- and medium-sized plants. For shrubs, trees, and other large plants, see "Number of Emitters per Plant Based on Canopy Diameter," page 80.

CONTROL SYSTEM WITH PRESSURE REGULATOR

An automatic microirrigation system is much like a sprinkler system; it requires backflow prevention and has remote-control valves on manifolds. However, each zone of a microirrigation system also needs a filter, a shut-off to facilitate cleaning the filter, and a pressure regulator.

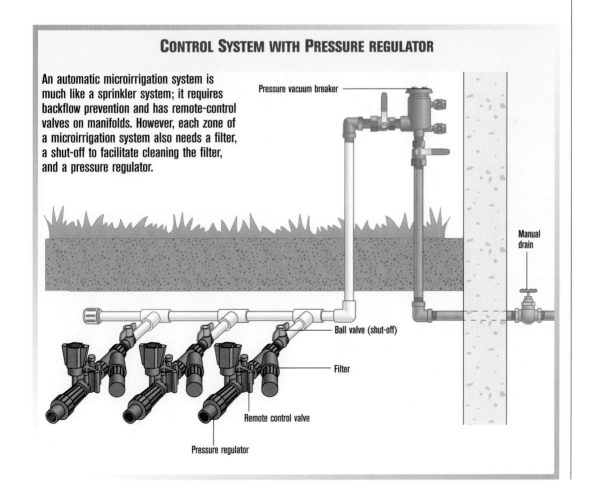

Pressure vacuum breaker

Manual drain

Ball valve (shut-off)

Filter

Remote control valve

Pressure regulator

WORKING WITH VINYL TUBING AND POLY PIPE

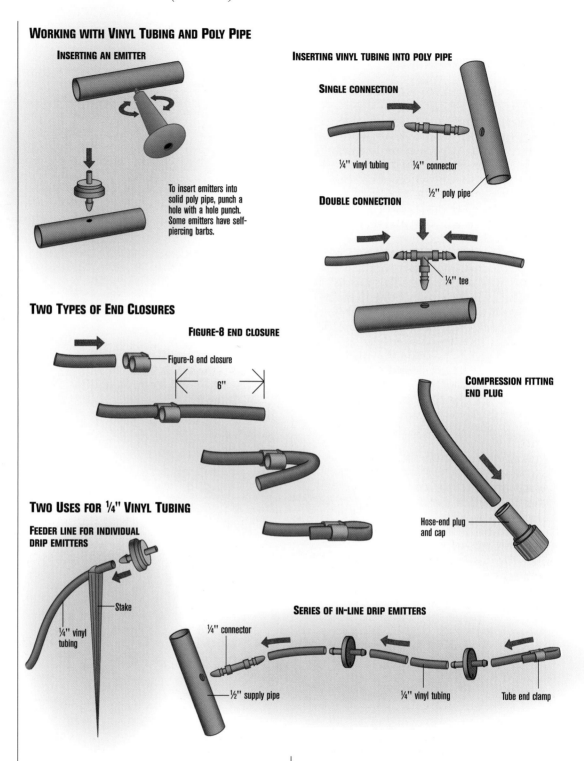

INSERTING AN EMITTER

To insert emitters into solid poly pipe, punch a hole with a hole punch. Some emitters have self-piercing barbs.

INSERTING VINYL TUBING INTO POLY PIPE

SINGLE CONNECTION

¼" vinyl tubing ¼" connector ½" poly pipe

DOUBLE CONNECTION

¼" tee

TWO TYPES OF END CLOSURES

FIGURE-8 END CLOSURE

Figure-8 end closure

6"

COMPRESSION FITTING END PLUG

Hose-end plug and cap

TWO USES FOR ¼" VINYL TUBING

FEEDER LINE FOR INDIVIDUAL DRIP EMITTERS

Stake

¼" vinyl tubing

SERIES OF IN-LINE DRIP EMITTERS

¼" connector

½" supply pipe

¼" vinyl tubing

Tube end clamp

Lateral-line installation

From here on, microirrigation installation is the same whether you use surface or subsurface supply lines. Start off by staking out the positions of the header lines, drain lines, and lateral lines. Next cut ½-inch poly pipe to the proper length and place it along the strings indicating its position.

■ **Installing parallel lines:** Header lines and drain lines require solid (unpierced) poly pipe. Some people prefer to use PVC pipe for both. Lateral lines, however, can be made of emitter line, porous pipe, or solid poly pipe to which you can then add emitters. Cut the header line as needed and insert tees or elbows where the laterals join it. If you've used compression fittings most

WORKING WITH VINYL TUBING

Inserting lengths of ¼- or ⅛-inch vinyl tubing as feeder line into ½-inch poly pipe is no more complicated than inserting a drip emitter. Just cut appropriate lengths of vinyl tubing with pruning shears or a knife, then punch a hole in the poly header pipe with a hole punch. Insert a barbed connector into the hole, then insert the other end of the barbed connector into the length of vinyl tubing. Where two sections of vinyl tubing must be attached at the same spot, used a barbed tee connector. If the vinyl tubing is too stiff, soak it in warm water before use. Do not use glue, oil, or lubricants to assemble the parts.

Each section of vinyl tubing can be connected to a single drip emitter or a series of in-line drip emitters. The drip emitter is simply inserted at the end of the section of tubing. An emitter should be held off the ground with a stake to keep it from clogging. In-line emitters are inserted by cutting the tubing at the appropriate spot, inserting the emitter, and pushing the tubing back into place around it.

Any section of tubing that does not end in a drip emitter should be plugged with a tube end clamp, which is used in much the same fashion as a figure-8 end clamp. Like all pipe, vinyl tubing must be flushed before installing end caps or terminal emitters.

To water trees or shrubs, space in-line drip emitters evenly along the line within the canopy area according to the number required (see chart on page 80). For other plants refer to Drip-Emitter Placement, page 87.

No more than 50 feet of ¼-inch tubing can be used in one zone and no more than 25 feet as lateral line. (Use ⅛-inch tubing only for very short runs.) Likewise vinyl tubing will support only a relatively small number of emitters—a total 15 gph. You could thus incorporate up to thirty ½-gph emitters or fifteen 1-gph emitters per zone.

INSTALLING MICROSPRINKLERS

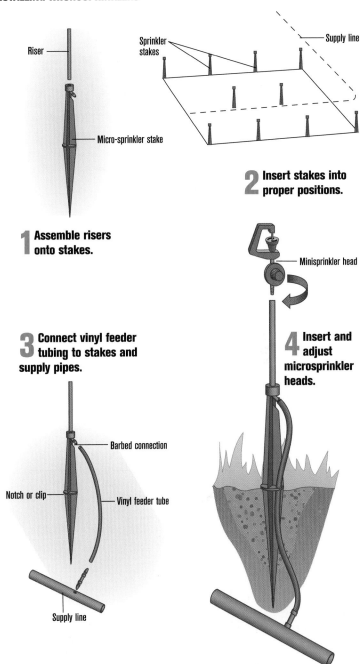

1 Assemble risers onto stakes.

2 Insert stakes into proper positions.

3 Connect vinyl feeder tubing to stakes and supply pipes.

4 Insert and adjust microsprinkler heads.

commonly supplied with microirrigation kits, assemble by simultaneously pushing and twisting the pipe into the fitting. For instructions on installing other kinds of connectors, see page 64. Now connect the lateral lines to the header line and flush until the water runs clear.

Next assemble the drain line at the opposite end of the laterals, in the same way as the header. Extend one line about 12 inches beyond the rectangle formed by the header and drainage lines for use as an end-closure extension. If you choose not to use a drain line, leave 12 inches of spare poly pipe at the end of each lateral line for an end closure. Flush again.

Install an end closure at each unattached lateral line. Figure-8 end closures are popular. To install, insert the end closure over the pipe, then bend back the end of the pipe and insert it in the other opening of the figure 8, pinching off the water circulation. A drawback of the figure 8 is that the bent section of the pipe may eventually crack. A hose-end plug costs more but is longer lasting. Insert the end of the lateral line into the compression fitting of the end plug. Screw the cap on or off as needed. Always place end closures at the lowest part in the system.

REPAIRING BLUNDERS

It is all too easy to accidentally punch a hole in the wrong section of pipe or, after testing the zones, to find one section that has too many emitters. This problem is easily corrected by cutting off the offending emitters and filling in the holes with hole plugs, often called goof plugs. Always have a few on hand when working with a hole punch.

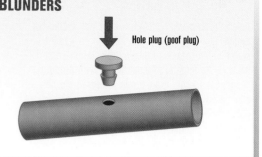

Hole plug (goof plug)

At this point drip emitters can be inserted into the lateral lines using a special hole punch. Formerly one emitter was placed at the base of each plant, but years of experience have shown that plants grow better when the entire root zone is kept evenly moist. To achieve this, space emitters regularly along the entire length of the lateral line rather than applying water to individual plants. Only where plants are spaced well apart should emitters be used at the rate of one per plant. The chart on page 87 gives suggestions for placement.

Installing lines for isolated plantings: Lay out the ½-inch poly pipe as determined in your plan, starting with the supply line, then the laterals, and finally any feeder lines, using tees and elbows as needed to connect the lines. Pin them down with plastic, metal, or wooden stakes, if necessary. Insert drip emitters within the lines as needed according to explanations given on page 81. Any sections that have no emitters can be buried 6 inches deep or more. Flush well. Terminate each unconnected line with an end closure.

Installing microsprinklers: Stake out the sectors to be watered using stakes or flags to represent the positions of the supply hose and the lateral lines. Assemble the sprinkler stakes. There is usually a thin riser that must be screwed or pressed into the top. Then sink the stakes lightly into the soil to mark the planned positions of the sprinklers.

Lay out the ½-inch supply line and assemble it with connector tees and elbows. It should be no farther than 5 feet from full-circle microsprinkler heads or 10 feet from half-circle, quarter-circle, or strip heads, because those are the limits for ¼-inch vinyl tubing, given the relatively high gph needs of microsprinklers. Cut the vinyl tubing to the length needed to reach from the stake to a convenient point on the ½-inch supply line, leaving a few inches of slack for adjustments.

Now punch a hole in the supply line with a hole punch, insert a connector in one end of the vinyl tubing, and plug the connector into the supply line. Attach the other end of the tubing to the barbed connection on the stake. Some stakes include a clip or notch into which the tubing can be slipped to prevent it from being yanked off the stake.

Turn on the supply line and flush until clean. Cap it with an end closure. Insert the appropriate type of microsprinkler into the top of each riser. Turn on the water again, and adjust the location and direction of the microsprinklers until you have complete coverage, then sink the stakes firmly into the ground. Depending on need, the supply line and lateral lines can be buried 4 to 6 inches below the ground or can be covered with mulch.

Hiding the lines: Once microirrigation is installed, the array of pipes can be unsightly, even if the nonemitting lines

INSTALLING MISTERS

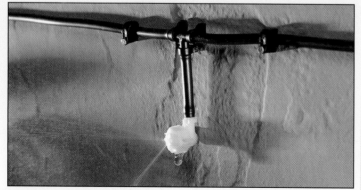

Although evaporative cooling misters use the same components as those used for hanging plants, avoid attaching them to the same zone.

Your watering system runs on a schedule; misters are used on-demand. Running both on the same system wastes water.

From water supply | ¼" vinyl lateral line | ½" supply line | ¼" vinyl tubing (lead-in) | End closure (at lowest end of zone)

were buried. As plants grow, their foliage will help hide the lines, but cover the lines with mulch in the meantime.

Decorative mulches do not block emitter outlets as soil can and therefore can be used to cover up emitter line, porous pipe, and any other landscape pipe that cannot be buried. Mulches come in a variety of textures, forms, and shades, from bark pieces to chopped cacao hulls to decorative stone. Mulches help decrease evaporation, thereby reducing watering needs, and encourage better plant growth. However, don't apply so much mulch that it prevents microsprinklers and other sprayers from reaching their entire zone.

Container gardens: a special case

Exposed to drying air and burning sun, container plants need more water more often than inground plants. Microirrigation is a perfect solution.

Drop by drop, day in and day out, automated microirrigation keeps the containers evenly moist. It is easily adapted to the plants' needs. If you like to move containers about, simply insert a hole plug in any unneeded tubing and punch into the supply line elsewhere.

Due to their special watering needs, container gardens should always be on their own zones. In many cases, you'll be watering daily, instead of every two or three days, and for shorter periods than other gardens.

Generally speaking, one or two drip emitters per container are sufficient, although long flower boxes may require three or more, set at about 12-inch intervals. If misters are used, only one is needed per container. Low-flow (½-gph) emitters are preferred, so water is applied slowly to avoid overflow, and they should be pressure-compensating, especially if hanging baskets are used in the zone.

Depending on conditions, leave on microirrigation for an hour or two, the time needed to moisten the mix entirely. When water begins to run out of the drainage holes, turn off the system.

Microirrigation may be efficient, but without proper planning it can be

NUMBER OF ½-GPH DRIP EMITTERS PER CONTAINER

Container Diameter	Number of Emitters
Up to 6"	1
7"–12"	2
13"–18"	3
19"–29"	4
Over 29"	1 every 6"

INSTALLING MICROIRRIGATION *(continued)*

SPECIAL WATERING SITUATIONS FOR CONTAINERS

HANGING CONTAINER

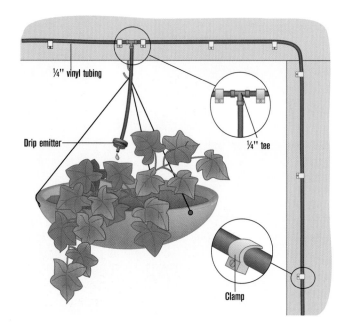

¼" vinyl tubing

Drip emitter

¼" tee

Clamp

LARGE CONTAINER

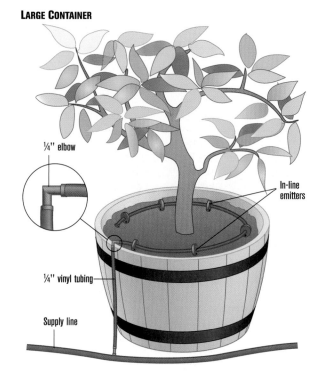

¼" elbow

In-line emitters

¼" vinyl tubing

Supply line

somewhat unsightly. Try running the supply line along the periphery of the growing space and behind the pots or even under a wooden patio. Vinyl tubing can be led up the back of the pots or even up

through a drainage hole before being clamped into place with a small stake. Rather than run a series of tubes up the back of the same container, use a section of ¼-inch tubing for a lead-in, then bend

▶ **Hanging containers are ideal candidates for microirrigation. Not only are they often difficult to water easily by hand, they dry out quickly. A drip or spray emitter can keep them flourishing.**

it into the pot with an elbow (See facing page). Place the tubing around the inside of the pot and insert in-line drip emitters about every 12 inches. Seal the end of the tubing with a hole plug or by inserting a drip emitter.

Watering hanging baskets requires more care. Run the line up the supporting structure in the least obtrusive spot, then across the top. Use ¼-inch vinyl tubing if possible, because it is easier to hide. However, it cannot be used in more than 25-foot lengths, so ½-inch poly tubing may be required as a lateral line. See page 89 for more information on working with vinyl tubing. Special support clamps for vinyl tubing and ½-inch pipe make it easy to fasten them, without crushing, to posts or masonry.

After installing microirrigation in containers, but before adding end-closure devices, turn on the water and flush the tubing thoroughly.

All container systems require adjustment over time. For one thing, as plants grow they require more water. You can leave the system on for a longer period, but that works only if the needs of all the containers increase at the same speed. Otherwise, add extra emitters or replace selected emitters with ones that provide a greater flow rate.

Another change comes with the end of summer, when watering requirements are reduced. Turn on the system for shorter periods. If any containers still get too much water, clamp off tubing or remove emitters and plug the holes.

In areas with freezing temperatures, drain the irrigation system in the fall. If possible disconnect it and bring it indoors for storage through the winter.

Vegetable gardens

Microirrigation is easily adaptable, so don't hesitate to use your ingenuity to find easy and practical solutions to your gardening needs. Vegetable gardens pose a particular challenge because their needs differ from those of other gardens in many respects. Don't throw away your hand sprinkler; newly seeded sections require hand watering until the seedlings are well-established.

Vegetable gardens should be on a separate zone where possible, because they need frequent, often daily, watering. Municipal regulations restricting watering usually allow you to water food plants as necessary. For a garden divided into several

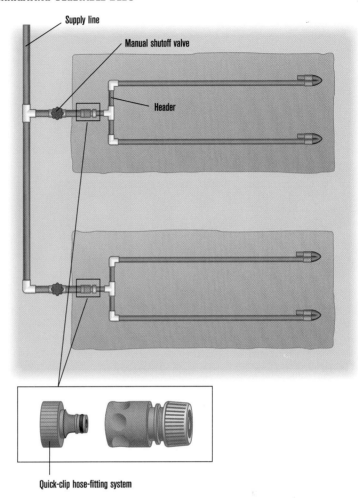

Quick-clip hose-fitting system

beds, it might be worthwhile to install a separate shutoff valve at the head of each one. Then you can open and close sections as their watering needs change—when one bed has sprouting vegetables yet others lie fallow, for example.

Vegetable gardens need frequent cultivation, which can damage irrigation lines. To get around this, use PVC pipe buried 18 inches deep as the supply line. Bring it aboveground with an elbow in a secure spot, and stake heavily so it is solid. Then set up the header and lateral lines using a quick-clip hose-fitting system, the kind used for changing rapidly from one hand sprinkler to another. This will require several adapters, but the result is a system that can be pulled out quickly whenever cultivation is required. In cold climates, bring aboveground sections indoors for the winter.

Using and Repairing an Irrigation System

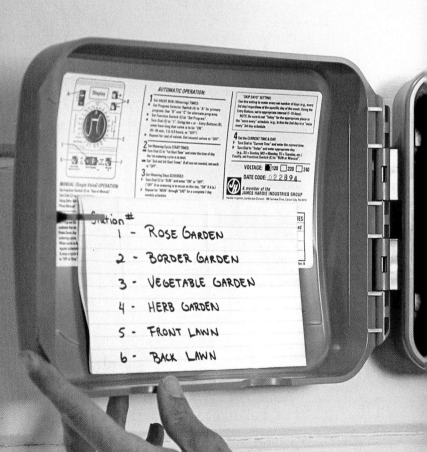

Once you have chosen the irrigation system you want, it's time to decide how you want to operate, maintain, and repair it. Will you control it manually by switching on the system yourself as you consult a graphed-out schedule, automatically with a programmed timer set to watering times and durations for each zone, or a combination of the two?

Once you've settled on your control method, you'll need to determine how much water to apply and when. This is not overly complicated, but it will require some

▼ **This weather-proof unit is wired into the home's electrical system through the junction box and conduit on the right. The conduit on the left conceals multiple-stranded, low-voltage wire that runs below ground to automatic sprinkler valves.**

time for figuring, testing, and adjusting before your system is running optimally.

Your irrigation system will need routine maintenance, especially at the beginning and the end of the watering season, to function at its best.

You may also find that watering needs change over time. When this happens, you may need to modify the system to accommodate the change. And of course, even in the best planned system, things can go wrong. If they do, consult the troubleshooting charts on pages 120–121.

USING YOUR SYSTEM

ROOT DEPTH AND EFFECTIVE WATERING

ABSORPTION ROOTS

SINKER ROOTS

1'
2'
3'
4'
5'

▼ The best time to irrigate is early in the morning, when still air and cool temperatures reduce evaporation, and warmth from the sun will dry off the plants.

N ow that your irrigation system is installed and operational, you still need to resolve a few questions. Just how automated do you want your system to be? How much and on what kind of schedule should you water? It will be easier to make these decisions if you first understand the following basic principles of watering.

How much to water

Overwatering wastes resources and can lead to diseased or rotted plants; underwatering stunts plant growth and can kill plants. The margin between those two extremes is, fortunately, broad. Most plants will grow and thrive when the soil varies between very moist and somewhat dry.

Old theories advocated watering to the point of saturation, then not watering again until soil was dry. With drip systems, especially, gardeners placed a few emitters near the base of a plant (instead of spacing them evenly throughout the garden, as is now recommended). They would run the system for hours, then allow the plant to dry out almost to the point of wilting before watering again. The result was irregular growth and considerable water loss, because much of the water went not to the plant but to rehydrate the soil.

The ideal situation is to keep soil moderately moist at all times to a depth of 1 to 2 feet. This upper layer of soil known as the root zone contains the most root hairs through which plants absorb water, minerals, and oxygen. There is no need to water to a greater depth; deeper-growing roots (sinker roots) serve mainly to anchor plants (see facing page).

To maintain moderately moist soil, run the system long enough to wet the root zone. How long this will take depends on the soil type and the rate at which the sprinklers put out water. Let the soil dry for five or more days before watering again. Because plants have different needs for water in different situations, become familiar with the plants in your landscape and develop a schedule that suits them best.

When to water

To irrigate properly, each of the zones in the yard must be on its own schedule. One of the reasons you divide the system into zones is to meet the individual needs of plantings. Only one zone can be operated at a given time without overloading the system. Zones can be run alternately, one coming on as another closes down, or on separate days, or even several times a day—depending on each zone's needs.

The ideal time of day to water is just before dawn. In the early morning, there is usually little wind to divert the water spray, and water pressure is at its maximum. Also, with the sun low in the sky, evaporation is slower so more water enters the soil and, therefore, the plants' cells than during the heat of the day.

Evening irrigation has two disadvantages. For one, water pressure is usually slightly lower at night. Of greater concern is the fact that diseases are more likely to infect susceptible plants when leaves remain moist through the night. With early morning watering, the leaves soon dry off as the day warms up.

The least efficient time to water is midday. On a hot, dry day, especially if it is windy, some of the water will evaporate before it enters the soil. In addition, sunlight can burn leaves covered with water droplets.

Since most microirrigation systems, especially those emitting water under ground or under a cover of mulch, do not produce a spray, there is less danger of water loss due to evaporation and less chance of burning or spreading disease. You can, therefore, run your microirrigation system at any time.

Manual systems

These are the most basic systems. You control the irrigation entirely without the aid of a timer, turning it on and off as needed. The main advantage of manual irrigation is that it keeps you in close contact with the yard and its needs. This contrasts strongly with an automatic system, which allows you to forget that occasionally human intervention might be useful. No automatic system yet created, for example, will turn off a sprinkler system on a windy day when much of the water will be blown onto the street. If you have a manual system, you might notice such water loss. You will probably also be aware that irrigation needs are less during cool weather. With an automatic system, you might not observe such changes.

A knowledgeable gardener can keep a watchful eye on all plantings and turn the water on and off as needed. Often a finger sunk into the earth daily will give all the information you need. If the soil feels dry to the touch, it requires watering; if it feels wet, it shouldn't be irrigated.

Manual systems are most practical when the yard is small or when only parts of it—

A manual-on, automatic-off valve uses a timer so it shuts off after a preset interval. This allows you to switch the system on at any time, safe in the knowledge that it will shut itself off.

▲ This hose-end system includes several timers and controls that allow you to preprogram watering in separate irrigation zones.

such as a vegetable garden—are irrigated. As the irrigated area increases in size and variety, running your system manually becomes more complicated.

Another major drawback to manual irrigation is your availability. To run such a system efficiently, you have to be available throughout the entire growing season and—given the watering restrictions in many towns and cities—often at odd hours of the day or night.

Manual-on, automatic-off

This is the most basic derivative of manual irrigation. You decide when to turn on the zone, but a simple controller turns it off. This is enormously practical if you want a manual system but are required by municipal regulations to run the system at night. You can turn it on before you go to bed and be assured that it will turn off the water as you sleep. It's also handy if you are the least bit forgetful. Many homeowners turn on the system, but then get busy with another task and forget to turn it off. This not only wastes water but could cause serious erosion problems and damage to plants and garden infrastructures. Manual microirrigation systems are particularly easy to forget, because there is often no outward sign that the system is running—until the basement begins filling with water.

Most automatic-off timers are simple and inexpensive and require no electrical hookup or batteries. Connect the timer to the system at any point after the control valve. Just twist the dial to set the length of time or the number of gallons.

Automatic watering

For people who travel a great deal or simply prefer the convenience of a system that runs itself, fully automatic timers are a necessity.

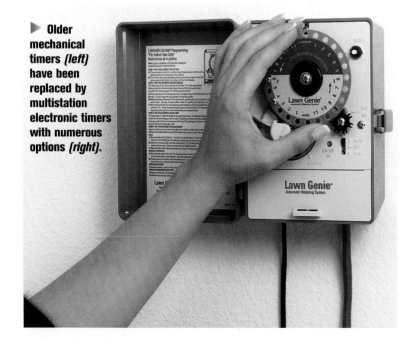

► Older mechanical timers *(left)* have been replaced by multistation electronic timers with numerous options *(right)*.

They take most of the effort out of watering and don't make demands on your time. And they are relatively inexpensive.

An irrigation timer is essentially a clock that tells the irrigation control valves to open and close at preset times, and to run for a preset number of minutes. It is possible to install an irrigation system without a timer, but the advantages of having one more than make up for the modest additional cost.

■ **Hose-end timers:** Hose-end timers, as their name suggests, mount directly to a hose fitting—normally a garden spigot. Traditionally they were controlled by a simple mechanical timer but have been supplanted by plug-in and battery-operated units. Because the hose-end system is so easy and flexible and well-suited for small urban yards, it has grown more popular in recent years. Manufacturers have responded with programmable hose-end timers that can control multiple irrigation zones.

■ **Programmable timers:** Programmable timers have become the norm for residential irrigation systems. Most have

similar capabilities and functions. The most widely available of these are multizone programmable timers.

Programmable timers are designed to be as autonomous as possible; once you have entered the irrigation scheduling

▲ **Push buttons on this programmable timer set up the watering schedule.**

ADDITIONAL TIMER OPTIONS

Multistation timers offer many options. Each additional option generally increases the price of the timer, so you will need to decide which are most vital to the correct organization of your irrigation system.

Make sure the model you choose is easy to program. Some are simple; others may seem as complicated as programming a computer from scratch. Have an irrigation dealer demonstrate a few models, then go back later and try to program them on your own.

A local dealer can be of enormous help in suggesting exactly which functions are most appropriate for your needs. Here are some of your choices.

■ **Station timing.** Most timers have both a minimum and a maximum run time. If you use emitters, where the zone often needs to run for several hours at a time, make sure you purchase a timer with station timing at least as long as the longest anticipated run time for your zone. At the other extreme, if you intend to use misters, remember they may need only a minute or so of irrigation at a time, so look for a timer offering short run times.

■ **Start times per day.** Some timers offer only one start time per zone per day. This may be sufficient for many microirrigation uses but not enough for sprinkler systems, especially those on slopes or clay soils that may need several short periods of watering during the same day. Other timers have ten or more start times per day, which is probably excessive for most needs but will be useful if you intend to use misters.

■ **Watering schedule.** There are dozens of possibilities: normal seven day weeks, odd/even-day intervals, one to thirty day intervals, etc. Seven-day schedules are sufficient when dealing with municipal

watering regulations, as they usually allow three watering days out of seven. Odd/even-day intervals, for watering every other day, usually suffice where such regulations don't exist. For situations in which a great deal of flexibility is required, such as systems with several very different zones, you can find timers that allow an almost infinite combination of schedules. Those with 365-day calendars make it possible to program the entire season in advance, including increased watering in dry months.

■ **Battery backup.** This feature makes sure your programming isn't erased during a power failure. Timers with 365-day calendars allow you to disconnect the timer for the winter and plug it back in during the spring; it has the program, current time, and date stored in memory and will be ready for action.

■ **Rain-off feature.** Most timers include a rain-off feature of some sort, which allows you to cancel watering when it rains. Some even allow you to program several days without irrigation, ideal when enough rain falls in one day to keep all plantings watered for a week.

■ **Manual override.** This feature allows you to water during times outside the normally programmed hours. It is useful for spot-watering and for spray adjustments and other verifications.

■ **Master valve circuit.** This circuit helps prevent water loss should something go wrong. A separate automatic valve will be needed as a master valve. This same circuit can also be used to activate a remote pump if the system requires one.

■ **Sensor functions.** These features allow the timer to override the programmed irrigation schedule when an attached sensor indicates no water is needed.

information, the timer will switch the various zones on and off at the times that you prescribed. Programmable timers are a major improvement on earlier mechanical timers because they can remember complex scheduling information and deliver water according to daily, weekly, or monthly cycles. The newest models even have 365-day calendars built into them, making it possible for them to deliver water in accordance with complex municipal watering schedules.

The timer interacts with the zone control valves the same way a mechanical timer would, sending an electrical signal to the valves telling them when to open and close. Most programmable timers can also be used to start irrigation pumps and open master valves. Many can make automatic adjustments based on information from rain and moisture sensors.

Be sure the timer you choose has the capacity to cover the number of zones that you've planned. It's a good idea to buy a timer that exceeds your current needs; an unused station or two makes it easy to add new zones later.

Programmable timers are fully electronic, with digital or liquid crystal screens for displaying your irrigation system program information. You begin by entering the time, the date, and the day of the week. Then manually enter the watering schedule for each zone.

Look for a timer that can run multiple programs, so you can put all your zones (or any combination of them) on different schedules, depending on plant needs, time of year, etc. With multiple programs, you can also have one set of zones watered

three times a week, another set watered once a week, and another watered on a different day. In any case, remember that only one zone can be running at any given moment.

■ **Software-based timers:** Like some cell phones, software-based timers will let you download information from a personal computer onto your irrigation system timer—information that can be used to manage all the details of your watering system. These timers promise to improve convenience and functionality dramatically.

Currently, software-based systems are available only with expensive and more sophisticated commercial irrigation timers (usually referred to as "controllers" when used for large-scale installations). These timers manage myriad watering schedules for extensive landscapes and automatically adjust each schedule, sometimes one sprinkler at a time. They use information fed to the timer, from the Internet and even from satellites, that provides real-time evapotranspiration data.

This kind of technology is on the horizon for homeowners. When it arrives, software for your home computer will interactively guide you through the process of creating a multizone watering schedule for your yard, which you can download into a timer. You'll be able to fine-tune zone parameters or watering needs as easily as you make corrections to a word processing document. In addition you'll be able to save as many programs as you like for future use.

■ **Rain- and moisture-sensing units:** These popular devices fill in one of the last gaps in automatic watering: They make sure that the system doesn't come on when water is not needed. Moisture sensors and automatic rain-shutoff devices override the timer to prevent irrigation; the only difference between them is how they do so. They are especially useful in climates where summer rainfall is frequent but variable. Wireless technology may soon make them easier than ever to install and use. Here are the types of sensors available.

Moisture sensors: These are inserted in the soil, where they measure the amount of moisture present. Many can be adjusted to different moisture levels, depending on the needs of the plants in the sector. They can usually be used to control one zone or several. The danger of controlling several zones with one sensor, however, is that irrigation needs usually vary; if your lot is irregular, a single sensor per zone is often

▼ **Moisture sensors make an automatic timer even more efficient.**

better. Also, even within a zone, there are areas that dry out more quickly or remain moist longer than others. You may have to experiment to find which sensor placement gives the most accurate general reading for the entire zone.

Automatic rain-shutoffs: Designed to measure rainfall rather than soil moisture, these devices are a popular choice where soil type is consistent and the property is of average size. A well-placed single rain-shutoff device can suffice for the entire yard. The unit operates by catching a small amount of rainwater. Electrodes then measure the water level. When the rainfall reaches a predetermined level, the unit cuts off the timer. Once the water level drops, the device lets your watering system resume its normal function. An automatic rain-shutoff should be placed in a spot that represents normal conditions for the sector that it controls: neither too shady nor too sunny, yet fully exposed to rainfall. Some units detect freezing temperatures as well to guard against unwanted runoff and ice buildup.

Moisture-sensor and rain-shutoff devices make irrigation easier, but they are not a panacea. You still may need to override the system manually under special circumstances and may often have to adjust the devices slightly to mesh with your

needs. Ask a local irrigation dealer which devices are best for your conditions. Some may be more reliable than others under your particular circumstances.

■ **Automatic control valves:** A multistation timer is useless unless it is connected to automatic control valves. Also called

▲ A rain-shutoff closes down the system during periods of rainfall. Similar units can detect freezing conditions as well.

WIRING FOR A TIMER

With multiple-stranded wire, it is easy to trace each zone from the control valve right through to the timer, making programming a snap.

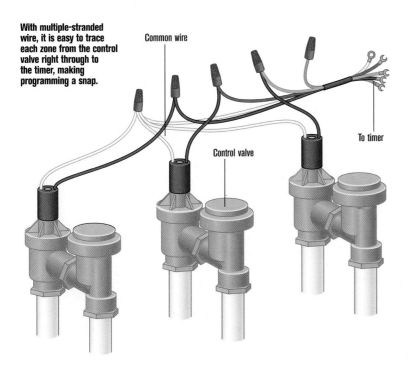

Common wire

To timer

Control valve

Connect wires with a wire connector (grease cap) designed for underground use. Connect one wire of each valve to the common wire; join the other wire to the colored wire designated for that zone.

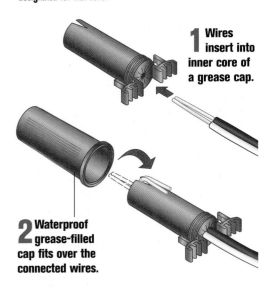

1 Wires insert into inner core of a grease cap.

2 Waterproof grease-filled cap fits over the connected wires.

HOOKING UP TO THE TIMER

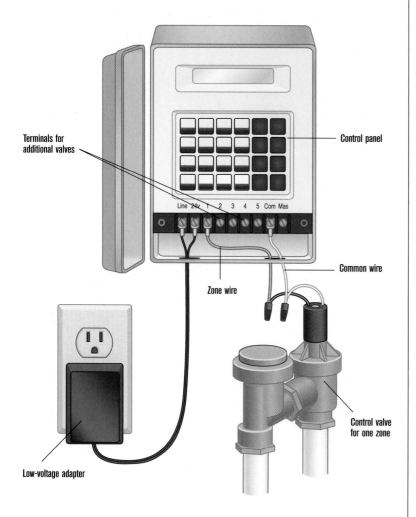

Terminals for additional valves

Control panel

Common wire

Zone wire

Control valve for one zone

Low-voltage adapter

remote-control valves, these include various kinds—in-line valves and antisiphon valves. They are designed to shut water on or off following an appropriate electronic impulse. The same type of automatic control valve can be used as both a master valve and a zone control valve See how to hook up a control valve on page 65.

If your system is new, put in automatic control valves as you install the piping, then use multiple-stranded wire to connect each valve to the multistation timer. Put in at least one strand more than the number of zones to use as a common wire and, if possible, one or two others for future zones. For line runs less than 800 feet long, you can use 18-gauge irrigation wire (sometimes referred to as plastic-jacketed thermostat wire). For longer runs use 14-gauge wire. The wire can be run along the trenches already dug for the piping, although it may

be necessary to dig a short, separate trench to lead the wires to the location of the timer. If possible lay the wire under the pipe, and make sure it is not touching any rocks or other abrasive material that might cut into the insulation. Wire should not be in contact with metal pipe; this increases the danger of current leakage and short circuits. If any wire will be in a trench by itself, especially in a garden area where digging might occur, run it through a length of PVC pipe to protect it from shovel damage.

It is easy to convert manual antisiphon valves to an automatic system. Turn off the water to the valves, remove the manual valve stem (but not the complete valve body) with a crescent wrench, and replace it with an appropriate automatic valve adapter. An irrigation dealer can help you select one suitable for your valve type. Then connect the adapters to the timer.

■ **Connecting the irrigation timer:** Locate a multistation timer in a dry spot that is readily accessible and near a power source. Many multistation timers are for indoor use only and are generally installed in the basement or garage. Others are built into weatherproof boxes and can be used indoors or out. It is sometimes cheaper to buy two smaller multistation timers than one larger one (four-, six-, and eight-station timers are standard); if so, you might like to locate the timers near the manifolds— one in the front and one in the back. If you have more than one timer, be careful to set them so that only one zone is in use at any one time.

Before connecting the wires leading from the automatic control valves to the timer, make sure the power is shut off to the timer. There will be two wires leading from each automatic valve. One is the zone wire, and it should be run to a numbered terminal screw on the timer. The other is the common, or ground, wire. In multiple-stranded wire, each wire has a different-colored plastic coating; choose a different color for the hot wire of each valve and one other color as the common wire. Attach each hot wire to a station in the timer box and note which wire color and station corresponds to which zone. Connect the common wires of the various valves and run only the one common wire to the common wire terminal screw of the timer. With some units you may need to attach the source lines from the plug-in power adapter. You can now plug in the timer and begin to program it.

WIRING A TIMER

Making the wiring connections at the timer is a relatively easy process. Although you may need a jeweler's screwdriver for attaching the wires to the wiring blocks of most timers, some manufacturers have begun using tool-free snap-in connectors to make the task easier.

1 Mount the timer and remove the terminal cover. Pull wires to the timer; fasten to the wall. If you used multi-color wires, you've got a head start on getting your connections right.

2 Strip each of the wires, removing ½ inch of insulation. Be careful not to nick the copper wire.

3 Connect the white wire to the COM terminal and begin attaching the valve wires.

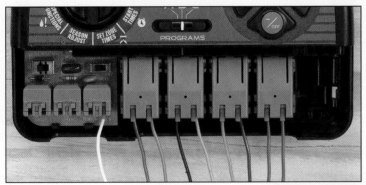

4 Connect the remaining colored wires to a terminal on the terminal block.

5 Complete the wiring by attaching the wires from the power source adapter. Plug the adapter into a receptacle.

Creating an irrigation schedule

The purpose of irrigation is to get the right amount of water to all the plants at the right time. To do so, you'll have to analyze the yard's needs, prepare a watering schedule, and adjust the schedule as needed.

■ **Sprinkler irrigation:** Many homeowners use instinct to work out an irrigation program. They simply turn the system on when they judge that plants need water, and off when the soil seems saturated. There's nothing wrong with this technique, but generally, plant growth will be uneven because this kind of care can't help but be slightly irregular. Also, if you automate the watering system, you will need to base your settings on something more than instinct.

You can develop an approximate watering schedule if you know a plant's average water requirements and your sprinkler output. For example, most lawn areas need about ½ inch of rain every other day. Most spray heads deliver ½ inch of precipitation in about 30 minutes; a rotary head can take three times as long, or 90 minutes, to deliver that amount of water.

With these estimates you could set up a fairly workable watering schedule, running the sprinklers every other day for 30 or 90 minutes. When the weather changes, you will need to revise the schedule. For example, in hot, dry weather, lawns may need up to an inch of water every other day. In cool weather, they need only about half the normal amount. You also sometimes have to factor in more than one irrigation session per day. For example, clay soils and slopes can't absorb ½ inch of water in 30 minutes. Instead it helps to apply ¼ inch in two separate sessions of 15 minutes, either on one day (leave at least 60 minutes between sessions) or on two different days. This calculation is a basic one because it considers only a few of the possible factors that affect, so be prepared to adjust the irrigation program if you find some zones are not getting enough water and others are receiving too much.

Precise ET scheduling: In very dry regions, such as areas west of the Rockies and in states such as Texas and California, homeowners are often advised to use ET, or evapotranspiration, rates as a basis for scheduling irrigation. Using local evapotranspiration information and a figure that approximates the water use of the plants in a yard, it is possible to arrive

▼ **Instead of a long watering, much of which runs off without soaking in, slopes need more frequent, less intense waterings.**

The irrigation checkbook resembles a regular checkbook. The deposits and withdrawals are made in water rather than money.

Day	Rainfall (deposit)	Irrigation (deposit)	Water Use (withdrawal)	Amount to Apply (balance)
	+1.05			1.05
1			-0.20	0.85
2			-0.20	0.65
3			-0.20	0.45
4		+0.45		0.90
			-0.20	0.70
5	+0.15			0.85
			-0.20	0.65
6	+0.38			1.03
			-0.20	0.83
7		+0.45		1.28

The irrigation checkbook can be precise and predictive, but it requires a lot of technical information and user management to keep it working properly.

at an accurate prediction of the water you will need to apply on a day-to-day basis for each irrigation circuit. If used correctly, ET scheduling can save 20 to 50 percent of average water use.

About ET: Evapotranspiration is a combination of the amount of water evaporated from plant leaves and soil and of the water transpired by plants through their pores. It is a measurement of the water used in the landscape.

ET is measured over time in inches. Wind, rain, temperature, humidity, and solar radiation affect the rate of ET. Evapotranspiration increases on days that are hot, dry, windy, or sunny. Cool, calm, cloudy, or humid conditions reduce evapotranspiration.

Historical ET rates—daily, weekly, monthly, and yearly—are available as are current measured rates. You can obtain this information from a local irrigation dealer, a cooperative extension agency, or, in some areas, from the weather bureau.

With historical rates, you might find, for example, that your region's ET rate is 7 or 8 inches per month in July, but only one-third that in November. It is important to adjust your controller each month to reflect seasonal and monthly ET rates.

ET checkbook: To understand the concept behind ET scheduling, it helps to think of a checkbook. The ET checkbook is similar to maintaining a checking account at the bank. Transactions are recorded regularly, perhaps even daily, using water as the currency. The correct balance for the account is established using precise information about soil properties and plant data that allow you to derive the correct water content for the soil for any type of plant. "Deposits" to the account include any precipitation—rainfall and irrigation—in inches. "Withdrawals" include water loss from the soil (evaporation) and how much water the plant actually uses (transpiration). The goal is to keep the actual water content of the soil as close as possible to the calculated optimal amount by balancing the deposits and withdrawals of water.

As a home irrigator trying to help your plants achieve ideal growth, you want to replace the water that is lost through evapotranspiration and not compensated for by rainfall. As a simple mathematical equation, irrigation equals evapotranspiration minus precipitation. Essentially, you add up the daily ET rates since the last time you watered, then subtract any rainfall deposits from the total ET to determine how much to apply.

ET controllers: At one time, homeowners and irrigation managers needed to make complicated calculations in order to set up ET-based watering schedules. Nowadays, several types of ET-based irrigation

PREPARING YOUR OWN IRRIGATION CHART

It is easiest to have an irrigation supplier work out a schedule for you, but if you want to do it on your own, here are the basics.
1. Find out the precipitation rate for each of your zones by using the chart supplied by the manufacturer for each type of head or emitter. For sprinkler systems, choose one of two rates usually given: square spacing or triangular spacing.

2. Determine the evapotranspiration rate per week for each month of the growing season for the region. You can get the rate per month from a county extension agent or the weather bureau. Divide this amount by 4 to get the rate per week.
3. Determine infiltration rate for each zone (see chart opposite).
4. Prepare a separate irrigation chart for each month.

IRRIGATION CHART

	Precipitation Rate (Precip. Rate) (inches/hour)	Evapotranspiration Rate (ET Rate) (inches/week)	Infiltration Rate (IF Rate) (inches/hour)	Total Weekly Irrigation Time (minutes/week)	Minutes Without Runoff	Number of Cycles Needed*	Number of Minutes per Cycle
	(According to manufacturer)	(Monthly ET Rate ÷ 4)	(See chart, on opposite page)	(ET Rate × 60 minutes ÷ Precip. Rate)	(IF Rate × 60 minutes ÷ Precip. Rate)	(Total Weekly Irrigation Time ÷ Min. without Runoff)	(Total Weekly Irrigation Time ÷ Cycles Needed)
Zone 1							
Zone 2							
Zone 3							
Zone 4							
Zone 5							
Zone 6							
Zone 7							
Zone 8							

Always round up this figure to the next highest number. For example, 4.1 would be 5.

Let's assume you have the following information:
1. The irrigation supplier gives you the precipitation rates for three zones: 0.5 inch per hour for zone 1; 0.8 inch per hour for zone 2; and 0.35 inch per hour for zone 3.
2. The evapotranspiration rate for the month is 5.4 inches. Divided by 4 this gives you a weekly rate of 1.35.
3. Your soil is a clay loam throughout the three zones and there

is no appreciable slope, giving you an infiltration rate of 0.25 inch per hour (see chart on opposite page).
Write in this information, then perform the calculations to complete the chart. Determine your schedule by adding the cycles needed per zone and the number of minutes of irrigation for each zone. Based on this information, the results for the first three zones are shown below.

IRRIGATION CHART EXAMPLE

	Precipitation Rate (Precip. Rate) (inches/hour)	Evapotranspiration Rate (ET Rate) (inches/week)	Infiltration Rate (IF Rate) (inches/hour)	Total Weekly Irrigation Time (minutes/week)	Minutes Without Runoff	Number of Cycles Needed*	Number of Minutes per Cycle
Zone 1	0.5	1.35	0.25	162	30	6 (5.4 rounded up)	27
Zone 2	0.8	1.35	0.25	101	19	6 (5.3 rounded up)	17
Zone 3	0.35	1.35	0.25	232	45	6 (5.1 rounded up)	39

controllers are on the market. Some allow you to manually adjust the watering times of all circuits with just one or two switches to reflect monthly changes in historical ET. More sophisticated models are hooked up by phone or satellite to a local weather station database and, for a fee, automatically adjust the schedule based on actual ET rates.

With an ET controller you will still need to determine an appropriate schedule for each circuit. You also must monitor the system to ensure no valves are stuck or sprinklers are clogged. Plus you should monitor whether your plants are faring well under the schedule. Be aware, too, that actual water savings will depend on the efficiency of your system.

■ **Microirrigation:** Water is applied slowly with microirrigation, so there is essentially no danger of runoff, not even on slopes or clay soils. This is important, because microirrigation usually runs for long periods. Most people find they can irrigate efficiently without doing any complicated calculations. Just ask an irrigation supplier what kind of irrigation program is recommended, or use the guidelines shown in the chart at the top of page 109.

You may need to increase the number of hours per irrigation cycle for trees and larger shrubs and decrease them for arid-climate plants as well as make adjustments according to your soil type. For information on timing the watering of container plants, see page 91.

■ **Easiest scheduling method:** The easiest way to come up with a precise watering schedule for each zone: Ask the irrigation supplier who drew up your plan to calculate it for you. The supplier should be able to estimate the number of times each zone on the system should be run per week and for how long, taking into account soil and irrigation type and the rate of precipitation of each zone. If you are working on your own, the chart on page 106 will help you calculate the number of cycles and the number of minutes to run each circuit.

Drawing up your schedule

Once you know how many irrigation cycles you'll need for each zone and how long each should last, decide when to run each cycle. There are two important factors here: Each cycle must run separately from all others, and if you intend to run a circuit for two or more cycles on one day, you must leave at least an hour between cycles. This allows the water from the first cycle to be absorbed by the time the second begins.

INFILTRATION RATE FOR LEVEL GROUND AND SLOPES

Average infiltration rate in inches/hour

Soil Texture Type	Percent of Slope				
	0–4.9%	5–7.9%	8–11.9%	12–15.9%	Over 16%
Coarse Sand	1.25	1.00	0.75	0.50	0.31
Medium Sand	1.06	0.85	0.64	0.42	0.27
Fine Sand	0.94	0.75	0.56	0.38	0.24
Loamy Sand	0.88	0.70	0.53	0.35	0.22
Sandy Loam	0.75	0.60	0.45	0.30	0.19
Fine Sandy Loam	0.63	0.50	0.38	0.25	0.16
Very Fine Sandy Loam	0.59	0.47	0.35	0.24	0.15
Loam	0.54	0.43	0.33	0.22	0.14
Silt Loam	0.50	0.40	0.30	0.20	0.13
Silt	0.44	0.35	0.26	0.18	0.11
Sandy Clay	0.31	0.25	0.19	0.12	0.08
Clay Loam	0.25	0.20	0.15	0.10	0.06
Silty Clay	0.19	0.15	0.11	0.08	0.05
Clay	0.13	0.10	0.08	0.05	0.03

USING YOUR SYSTEM *(continued)*

You can water daily, every second day, three times a week, or whatever interval is appropriate, as long as each zone gets its required precipitation during that period. However, it is better to water each zone deeply a few times a week than lightly every day. Many people prefer to limit their irrigation cycles to two or three days a week.

To visualize the watering schedule before posting it on a wall for manual irrigation or programming it into the automatic controller, draw up a chart (see page 104). It should include the days of the week and the times when each zone should be turned on and off. If local watering restrictions apply, you must irrigate only on the days and at the times permitted.

Once you have determined the watering days, start times, and run times necessary to get the proper amount of water on the ground in each zone, draw up a schedule. You'll need such a schedule whether you are going to program a timer or run the irrigation system manually.

Graph paper is not essential, but it will make drawing your schedule much easier. In addition have on hand a ruler and a few colored pencils or markers.

■ **Mark the columns:** Divide the paper into eight equal columns. Label the first column "Time." Label the remaining columns with the days of the week.

"FERTIGATION"

Golf courses, sports fields, and nurseries, routinely use irrigation systems to feed plants. This is an efficient feeding method, but so far, it's not proven practical in home systems. With microirrigation, however, you may be able to use a device like the one shown here. Check with your local dealer to see if fertigation would work with your system.

FERTILIZING AUTOMATICALLY

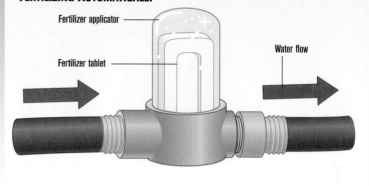

Fertilizer applicator

Fertilizer tablet

Water flow

▼ **Drawing out your schedule makes it simple to operate your manual system or correctly program your automatic timer.**

■ **Indicate the time intervals:** Mark the "Time" column with the hours of the day. It is usually enough to break the hours into no more than 10-minute sections; little is gained by smaller intervals. Leave out the mid-day hours when the sun is too intense for watering.

WATERING GUIDELINES FOR MICROIRRIGATION SYSTEMS		
Weather	**Duration in Hours**	**Number of Times Per Week**
Cool	2	1 or 2
Warm	3	2
Hot	4	3

Time" column in the Irrigation Chart on page 106). It becomes clear in the sample schedule that it won't be necessary to water on all three permitted days, because only about 8½ hours of irrigation are needed, yet 18 are available. Because deep waterings are preferable to frequent shallow ones, irrigations are concentrated on only two days, Monday and Thursday. The six cycles required for each zone can, therefore, be divided into three cycles for each of the watering days.

■ **Making adjustments:** After you have lived with your system for a few weeks, you'll probably find that minor tweaks are needed. Spray heads may need adjustment (see page 113) to make sure they aren't

▲ **Large shrubs may need increased hours of irrigation.**

■ **Show blackout periods:** If local watering restrictions apply, indicate the unavailable watering times on your schedule. Shading them in is a good idea to avoid watering during restricted times by mistake. In our sample watering schedule *below*, watering is allowed only on Tuesdays, Thursdays, and weekends between 5 p.m. and 6 a.m.

■ **Show start times:** Mark the start times you have chosen to use on each day by drawing a line across your chart at the correct times for each day.

■ **Color-code the zone run times:** One by one, mark out the run times for each zone. For clarity and readability, use a different colored pencil or marker for each of the zones in the system. Draw a line that corresponds to the run time for that zone.

Post this schedule at the control valves if you will be operating the system manually, or use it to program your automatic irrigation timer. Leave a copy of it near the timer for easy reference later.

The sample watering schedule *(right)* is for a municipality that limits watering to Mondays, Wednesdays, and Thursdays between midnight and 6 a.m.

In this example water restrictions apply; the first step is to compare the hours when watering is permitted with the total number of hours of irrigation required by the zones (this is calculated by adding up the figures in the "Total Weekly Irrigation

SAMPLE WATERING SCHEDULE

	S	M	T	W	T	F	S
First Cycle							
Zone 1		12:00–12:27			12:00–12:27		
Zone 2		12:28–12:45			12:28–12:45		
Zone 3		12:46–1:25			12:46–1:25		
Second Cycle*							
Zone 1		1:27–1:54			1:27–1:54		
Zone 2		1:55–2:12			1:55–2:12		
Zone 3		2:25–3:04			2:25–3:04		
Third Cycle*							
Zone 1		2:54–3:21			2:54–3:21		
Zone 2		3:22–3:39			3:22–3:39		
Zone 3		4:04–4:43			4:04–4:43		

* Note that the second and third cycles don't start until one hour after the previous cycle is completed. An automatic system will not repeat irrigation on the same zone until one hour has elapsed to allow time for the water to soak into the soil. For example, the first cycle of Zone 1 ends at 12:27 a.m., and the second cycle doesn't begin until 1:27 a.m.

USING YOUR SYSTEM (continued)

▶ **The fastest way to make sure your sprinkler heads are aligned is to put on rain gear and adjust them while the system is running.**

▼ **A few simple calculations will help you take the guesswork out of scheduling sprinklers.**

wasting water by spraying walks, patios, and driveways. This adjustment is often best done while the system is running *(left)*.

You'll probably need to make minor adjustments in the irrigation program as well. Some zones may need longer or more frequent irrigation sessions than originally planned, and others less. Adjust the programming until plants are getting enough water and no puddles or excess runoff develops.

You will also need to adjust according to weather conditions. During unseasonably warm periods, manually override an automatic system and add a watering period. Under cooler-than-average conditions, you might skip a watering.

Any precipitation will also affect watering needs. If you haven't installed a rain sensor (see page 101), you may want to use a rain gauge to check how many inches fell, then subtract that amount from the month's evapotranspiration rate to see how many irrigation cycles to skip. However, bear in mind that plants that are growing extremely rapidly may need longer or more frequent irrigations.

A catch-can test (facing page) is an excellent way to check and adjust coverage.

The catch-can test is a simple and effective way to check the performance of your sprinklers once they are all in place and working. Doing this test will let you know that your system is watering as planned and help you determine whether your irrigation schedule will have to be adjusted to create the most efficient watering cycles for your yard.

To do the test, you will need a number of containers of the same size and shape. They should have a flat bottom and vertical sides—using containers with sloping sides will throw off the measurements you get from the test. Soup cans or coffee cans work well for this; anything shorter allows too much water to splash out. Space the containers in a grid pattern throughout the zone being checked. All the containers should be equidistant from one another.

Don't worry if you don't have enough cans to cover the entire test area; you can perform the test in one area, then move the cans to another area to complete the test.

Once the containers are in place, turn on the irrigation system and let it run for exactly 15 minutes. Then turn off the system and measure the depth of the water in each container. Add those amounts together and divide the total by the number of containers to get the average amount of water for each. Multiply that by 4 to calculate the precipitation rate of your irrigation system in inches per hour.

You can use different run times, but you will have to multiply your measurements by something other than 4. For instance, if you let the system run for 10 minutes, you will multiply your average per can by 6 to get the rate in inches per hour.

If you notice a large difference in the amount of water in the different cans, you know that you will need to adjust the sprinklers in that area to create matching coverage. Make the adjustments, then run the test again. You may have to do the test and make adjustments several times before getting the coverage right.

▲ Doing a catch-can test is an easy way to double check your irrigation system's performance, and the only way to know how even your coverage really is.

▲ After running the zone being tested for 15 minutes, use a ruler or tape measure to measure the depth of the water in the container.

PERFORMING ROUTINE MAINTENANCE

Properly designed irrigation systems require only minimal maintenance. However, a little upkeep is vital. And as time passes, you may find that you want to adapt your system to changing needs.

Checking system operation

At installation time and at the beginning of each season, check the system thoroughly. Turn on each zone individually and make sure the water is reaching all areas it is supposed to cover. Most adjustments are easy to make. During the season simply keep an eye open for problems. Some of the signs that the system needs minor adjustments are spray reaching unwanted parts of the yard, areas that remain dry after spraying, and excessive puddling or runoff.

Visual checks are easiest to make with sprinkler systems, because it is simple to see how they are spraying and if the water is reaching the intended areas. Microirrigation needs more careful attention. You may have to get down on your knees and push aside a bit of mulch to be sure that water is indeed dripping from each nozzle. Subsurface emitter lines and porous pipe systems are more difficult to verify, because the soil can be completely dry on the surface yet moist underneath. Puddles

of water on the surface can indicate leaks, overly long watering periods, or pressure problems. Sectors where plant growth is stunted or withered while nearby areas are green and growing could indicate a plugged emitter or a pinched pipe. Finally, check any moisture sensors annually.

Cleaning and flushing

All irrigation systems need to be cleaned occasionally to remove dirt, debris, or plant materials that have built up over the seasons. Take some time now to review these procedures to ensure that water can run freely through your irrigation system.

■ **Sprinkler systems:** Dirt and debris can accumulate in the pipes, risers, and nozzles of a system. To prevent buildup, flush out the system at least once a year. With the system turned off, remove individual nozzles and heads, then turn on the water for a few minutes until a clean, solid stream flows from each head. Turn off the water. Take apart the nozzles (depending on the type, this can be done by hand or with a screwdriver, or a special key may be needed) and clean them to remove any dirt. Rinse out the screen or filter basket as well. Reassemble and replace all the parts. Turn on the zone again to check that everything is operating properly.

▼ **The supply line for a new valve should be flushed out before the valve is installed.**

Make sure you keep the lawn mown around stationary and pop-up lawn heads so grass won't block the spray. You may occasionally need to prune vegetation growing around spray heads in garden, groundcover, and shrub areas.

■ **Microirrigation systems:** Microirrigation systems are more sensitive to blocking by dirt and debris than spray systems are, so they should be cleaned more frequently. Once a month during the operating season, remove the end closure from each line and flush the line thoroughly until the water runs clear, then put the end closure back in place.

Flush the filter monthly. Most can be flushed simply by turning on the flush outlet (dump valve). Otherwise, take out the filter and rinse it. Even filters that have a flush outlet should be taken apart, cleaned, and inspected at least once a year. If the screen inside shows any sign of damage, replace it.

Adjusting for coverage and spray

At installation and at the beginning of each season, as well as during the season if there is an obvious problem, check for proper coverage from each spray head. The heads may have been knocked out of alignment by a careless footstep, a wayward lawn mower, or a snow shovel. This can cause them to spray sidewalks or other unintended surfaces while leaving part of

◀ **For many sprinkler heads, a screwdriver is the only tool you need to make adjustments.**

the garden unwatered. There might also be too much or not enough overlap between heads. To make adjustments, either remove the nozzle to redirect its spray, turn the flow-adjustment screw on the top of the nozzle, or use a special ratchet. Most rotary heads have a friction collar at their base

◀ **Use an air compressor to clear sprinkler lines before the winter freezes.**

ADDING TO AN ESTABLISHED SYSTEM

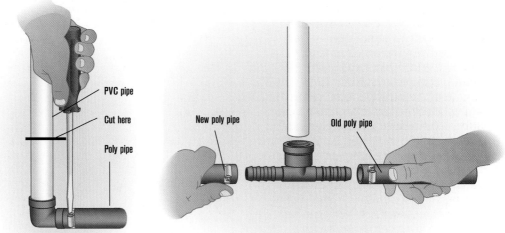

PVC pipe

Cut here

Poly pipe

New poly pipe

Old poly pipe

1 Cut the PVC pipe above the fitting. Unscrew the clamp and remove the poly pipe.

2 Add a combination tee and attach the new poly pipe and the old poly pipe.

that can be used to adjust the angle and a diffuser screw to adjust the distance of the throw. With microsprinklers, you can simply twist the head to change its direction.

Sometimes spray heads produce a mist or fogging action rather than the large drops necessary. This indicates the water flow is too strong; it can be adjusted easily at the zone control valve. If the system is manual, turn the system shutoff clockwise until you see large drops. Automatic valves have a special knob for this adjustment.

Winterizing

Although some manufacturers claim their systems can withstand freezing conditions if automatic drains are installed at the lowest point in each zone, thoroughly draining the system each winter is always worthwhile in freezing climates. To do so, drain all water from the zone by turning off the main valve and running each zone for a few minutes. Next, blow any remaining water from the control valves using an air compressor (compressors usually can be rented). Repeat for each zone until the entire system is clear of water. It's best to bring any aboveground sections of a microirrigation system indoors for the winter. In spring when the ground

ADDING A NEW PVC LINE

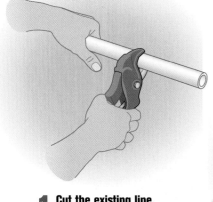

1 Cut the existing line.

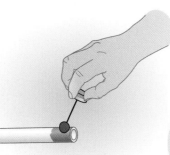

2 Apply primer to the pipe ends and the inside of the fitting, then apply cement.

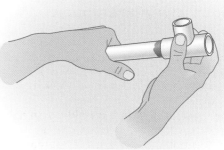

3 Attach the tee, making sure it is pointing in the right direction.

has completely thawed, reinstall any microirrigation piping removed the previous fall, turn the main valve back on, and check out the system carefully (see page 112).

Disconnect stand-alone timers and bring them in for the winter. Unplug multistation timers and remove the battery, unless the battery keeps the timer programmed for the entire winter. Replace the battery with a new one each spring.

Adapting to changing needs

Your garden will probably change and so will its watering demands. Often you may need only to readjust the watering schedule or adjust the flow of sprinklers, but if you've added new beds or radically altered the use of any part of the yard, you must make more significant changes.

Modifications to aboveground microirrigation systems are easy to carry out, especially if you left room on each zone for future additions. Just add line and punch in new emitters. You can also replace emitters and microsprinklers with some of higher or lower output (or, in the case of microsprinklers, of a different pattern). Just be sure to recalculate the zone's capacity before adding any component to avoid overloading the zone. If you remove any lines or emitters, simply install hole plugs as shown on page 90. Subsurface microirrigation installations require digging, of course, but the process is otherwise similar.

Adding modifications to sprinkler systems is not complicated if you left space on each zone for future development, but some digging will generally be necessary. Before adding an extra sprinkler head or pipe to a zone, check that enough pressure is available on the zone. Dig carefully so you don't break the pipe or other fixtures already in place; then dig whatever trenches are necessary for the new section.

See pages 59–71 to learn how to install new pipe and fixtures. Any PVC fittings that are cut out as you make changes will have to be replaced; once cemented in place a joint is permanent. Polyethylene fittings, however, can be removed and usually are in good enough shape to be reused. Spray heads and risers can also be used again.

Sometimes modifying a sprinkler system is as simple as changing a few sprinkler heads or even just the nozzles. With many modern sprinkler heads, for example, a full-circle nozzle can be replaced with a

part circle or even a strip nozzle in a matter of seconds. When lawn sections are converted into shrub or flower beds, sometimes the change is as simple as placing the lawn sprinkler heads on higher risers. Be certain, however, that any sprinklers added or changed will be compatible with others on the zone. You couldn't convert, for example, only two rotary heads on a zone to spray heads.

Any major changes could require the addition of a new zone. Once again, the process is much easier if you left space in the original system—for example, a manifold sealed with a cap rather than an elbow, or a timer with at least one extra station.

▲ Adjustable risers can be raised as shrubs and bushes grow, and lowered after a pruning.

▼ A collection of microirrigation parts makes it easy to adjust your system to new plantings.

REPAIRING THE SYSTEM

Fortunately, little can go wrong with a properly installed irrigation system. Malfunctions are the exception rather than the rule. If something does go wrong, here's how to diagnose the problem.

Troubleshooting your system

To discover the cause of irrigation system malfunctions, consult the troubleshooting charts on pages 120–121. Most potential problems can be noted and corrected during routine maintenance. Regular flushing and cleaning, especially of filters and sprinkler heads, will eliminate most problems before any serious damage is done. Some problems may need more vigorous intervention.

■ **Locating leaks:** Leaks are the most pernicious of irrigation problems. They can go unnoticed for long periods, and often the only symptom of a minor leak is that the system operates less and less efficiently over time. Only when the problem becomes more serious does water buildup saturate the ground, a sign there is a leak in the sector.

REPAIRING PVC PIPE WITH A REPAIR COUPLING

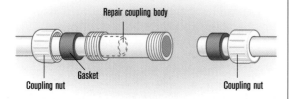

Repair coupling body

Gasket

Coupling nut

Coupling nut

REPAIRING PVC PIPE BY REPLACING DAMAGED SECTION

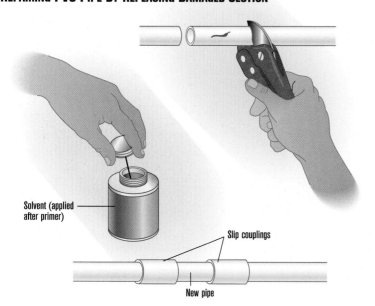

Solvent (applied after primer)

Slip couplings

New pipe

If you suspect a leak in an aboveground section of a zone (this is likely only with microirrigation), the source of the problem is easy enough to trace. Remove any mulch, turn on the zone, and check for any unwanted bubbling or spraying.

Leaky sections of underground pipe are much harder to locate. When a leak is suspected in a high-pressure irrigation system, cap off all the spray heads, turn on the zone, and wait until the appearance of surface water indicates where the leak is located. If you can't find the leak, call in a professional who can use special equipment to trace it. Otherwise, you will have to dig, and without knowing where to begin, you may unearth much of the system before finding the leak.

■ **Repairing pipe damage:** Improper seals of poly-pipe joints can be corrected simply by tightening the clamps where the leak occurs. Small leaks in poly or PVC pipe can be repaired easily with a hole plug or with a repair coupling, also called a dresser coupling. To install a repair coupling *(left)*, turn off the water and use plastic-pipe shears or a hacksaw to cut through the pipe at the leak. Then part the two pipe ends far enough to slip on the repair coupling components, center the coupling body over the cut, and tighten the coupling nuts and gaskets until firmly in place.

Major leaks in poly, PVC, or any other kind of pipe mean that the damaged section must be replaced *(below left)*. It is best to insert an additional length of pipe wherever connections have been pulled apart, because this kind of damage, often the result of deep frost causing the line to contract, is likely to recur. Leaks in PVC pipes, unlike those in poly pipe, can be repaired only by replacing the damaged section. Repairing pipe is as simple as cutting out the damaged section and inserting new pipe and joints (see page 64).

Always turn off the water before making repairs; then check the system and flush it thoroughly before reburying the pipe. Poly-pipe fittings near damaged sections can be reused if they are still in good condition, but don't attempt to repair fittings near damaged PVC pipe: Just cut them out and replace. Poly pipe can also be pinched by kinks along its length or by stones or rocks pressing into it. If so, part of the zone will fail to operate. Dig up the zone, starting from the last fully functioning spray head or emitter, and straighten the kink or remove the obstruction. The pipe should be buried in sand to prevent further blockage. Test the zone before covering the pipe again.

■ Correcting valve problems: Modern valves are less subject to sticking than older ones and are much easier to adjust. Problems with excess or insufficient flow (see chart on page 120) are easily corrected by adjusting the flow control. Each model has a different type of control, but most are easily adjusted by hand with a wrench or a special key. Leave the zone running as you turn the flow control so you can check results. You may need a helper to report on the results if the spray head is not visible from the control valve.

When a zone won't open or doesn't shut off automatically, there may be a problem with a control valve. Try opening and closing the valve rapidly while the water is running to dislodge any dirt. If that fails, turn off the water and take the valve apart according to the manufacturer's directions, removing any debris or buildup and looking for cracks or other damage. Often the problem is an overly tightened flow control. Before reinstalling the valve stem, lubricate it according to the manufacturer's instructions. Cracked or damaged control valves can sometimes be repaired but are best replaced with new ones.

When a manual control valve is hard to turn or sticks, see if the threads on the valve stem have been damaged (this can happen if the valve stem was installed improperly). If so replace the valve stem. If none of the zone operates, check the main control valve. You may simply have forgotten to turn it on after the system was closed down for the winter. Or it could be faulty and require cleaning or replacement, as explained earlier. Automatic valves not opening or closing properly may also be due to a damaged timer.

■ Diagnosing timer problems: Automatic irrigation systems that depend on the efficient operation of the timer are subject to a number of problems, most due to faulty wiring. When the circuit breaker controlling an automatic irrigation system trips or when valves fail to open or close, even though the valves have been thoroughly cleaned and inspected, the cause is generally a poor wire connection or a shorted wire. Make sure the circuit breaker is off and check all wire connections, including those at the automatic timer, zone valves, and main valve. Repair any that look faulty. Make sure the connections are properly sealed and waterproofed. Water in contact with

SERVICING IRRIGATION VALVES

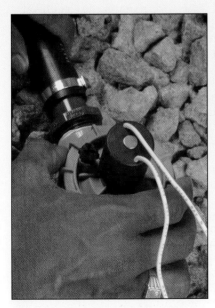

After turning off the power, remove the hold-down ring by removing the screws or unthreading it.

Remove the valve bonnet and spring. Then carefully pry out the diaphragm and flush the valve body with water.

Gently push the new diaphragm into its seat. Then reassemble the valve and test for leaks.

▲ One of the best preventive maintenance routines you can do for your drip-irrigation system is to rinse and inspect the mesh filter every year. Replace it at the first sign of wear.

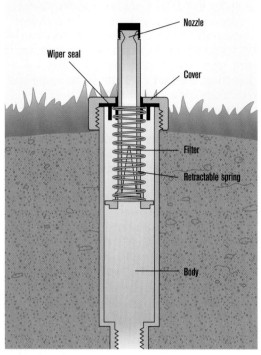

a bare wire is a common cause of system malfunction. If the connections seem intact, you may need to dig up part of the inoperative zone to trace the location of a break in the wire.

Preventing spray head and emitter problems

The careful and regular cleaning of your system (see page 112) will prevent most spray head and emitter problems. Make certain that nozzles and emitters are washed; that filters are cleaned and, if necessary, replaced; and that the zone is flushed regularly.

Pop-up spray heads present special problems. If they refuse to pop up or retract, the problem is usually the wiper seal, a rubber or plastic gasket designed to keep dirt out of the spray head (see *above right*). When this gasket wears out, small particles of dirt can jam the pop-up riser in place. Remove the nozzle (check the manufacturer's instructions) and clean it. If the wiper seal appears worn or torn, replace it. In older pop-up heads especially, springs tend to rust and may need to be replaced.

Soil often builds up over the years, especially in turf areas, obstructing heads more and more until they no longer irrigate

efficiently. When buildup occurs, simply dig around the head, down to the main pipe, flush thoroughly, then turn off the zone and replace the riser with a taller one. Flush again before you reinstall the spray head. If you chose adjustable risers to start with, they can be adjusted to the new height by twisting.

SPRAY HEAD MAINTENANCE

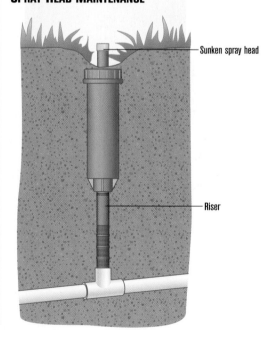

Servicing sprinklers

Regular inspection of your sprinklers will prevent most spray head problems. Make sure that nozzles and filters are clean and replaced when damaged or worn out. Don't be surprised to find that filters have not been installed on your sprinklers as they should be. Missing filter baskets are responsible for many a clogged sprinkler nozzle.

The other major mechanical reason a pop-up sprinkler won't pop is a damaged riser-retraction spring. If the riser has no spring tension at all, the entire sprinkler should be replaced. Do not open the sprinkler body.

Due to safety concerns over the danger of the riser-retraction spring being ejected from the sprinkler body, it is no longer possible to replace the wiper seal yourself. If it goes bad, you will need to replace the entire sprinkler body. This is one more reason why it pays to keep this area of the sprinkler clean and free of dirt or debris.

Any repair that requires opening the sprinkler body, or repairing connections to it, will require that you take the sprinkler out of the ground.

REPLACING A POP-UP SPRINKLER HEAD

1 Dig out all the dirt from around the head so you have access to the head and the riser or the connection beneath. Reach under the sprinkler head with one hand and hold onto the riser or tee connection at the base of the sprinkler.

2 With your other hand, loosen and unscrew the sprinkler from the riser. Avoid getting dirt get into the riser or tee as you remove the sprinkler head.

3 Thread the new or repaired head onto the riser, and tighten it hand-tight plus a quarter to half turn. Be sure to hold the pipe beneath it to stabilize it. No pipe dope or tape is needed with these plastic fittings.

REPAIRING THE SYSTEM *(continued)*

TIMER TROUBLESHOOTING

Symptom	Cause	Solution
The watering cycle repeats.	Too many start times.	Disable redundant starts.
	Season adjust is set at more than 100 percent.	Set the season adjust to 100 percent or less.
The fuses blow too often.	Valve solenoid is faulty.	Replace the solenoid.
	Wires to valves are damaged.	Repair the wiring.
	Timer is faulty.	Replace the timer.
The timer's display is blank.	No power to the timer.	Check the outlet for power.
	Transformer is faulty.	Replace the transformer.
	Popped circuit breaker or blown fuse to the timer.	Repair damaged wiring or replace the bad solenoid.
	Timer is faulty.	Replace the timer.
The irrigation system does not water the yard.	Timer is off, or it has a blown fuse.	Replace the fuse and turn on the timer.
	No power at outlet.	Reset the circuit breaker.
	No 24-volt power from transformer to timer.	Replace the bad wiring or the transformer.
	Wires to valves are damaged.	Repair any damaged wiring.
	Faulty transformer, timer, or rain sensor.	Replace any faulty components as needed.
	Incorrect start times, run times, or watering days.	Check timer program settings.
The circuit is not working.	Damaged circuit connection.	Repair the wiring.

VALVE TROUBLESHOOTING

Symptom	Cause	Solution
A zone valve will not turn on.	Incorrect start times, run times, or active days.	Check the timer program.
	Water supply to the zone valve is off.	Turn on the water supply.
	Faulty valve solenoid.	Replace the solenoid.
	Closed control at valve.	Open it counterclockwise.
A zone valve will not turn off.	Zone valve wires are not connected.	Connect the wires.
	Timer programming is incorrect.	Check the timer program.
	Debris in valve, solenoid, or metering orifice.	Disassemble the valve and clean with fresh water.
Water is leaking from a valve.	Valve diaphragm is faulty.	Replace the valve diaphragm.
	Valve body is cracked or broken or the valve bonnet is broken.	Replace the valve.
Leak occurred from lowest sprinkler in zone.	Damaged valve diaphragm.	Replace the diaphragm.
A manual valve is stuck or hard to operate.	Dirt in the valve.	Clean and lubricate the valve stem.
	Damaged threads on stem.	Replace the valve stem.
Misting of the spray occurs.	Flow is too high.	Adjust the flow control on the irrigation valve.
The spray pattern is too small.	Flow control is set too low.	Adjust the flow control to increase the water flow.

MICROIRRIGATION TROUBLESHOOTING

Symptom	Cause	Solution
There is no water coming from an emitter.	The emitter is clogged.	Clean the emitter or replace it.
One part of the drip zone is dry.	Not enough emitters in that area.	Add emitters or replace with higher-flow emitters.
	Kinks in the poly tubing.	Inspect the lines and straighten if needed.
Part of the zone is too moist.	Too many emitters in that area.	Reduce the number of emitters in that area, or replace them with lower-flow emitters.
Emitters come loose .	Too much pressure in the system.	Add a pressure regulator to the line.
Container plants are too dry.	Not enough irrigation.	Add more emitters; or put containers on a separate zone; increase irrigation time.
Container plants are too wet.	Too much irrigation.	Remove emitters; or put containers on a separate zone; decrease time.

Sprinkler Troubleshooting

Symptom	Cause	Solution
The sprinklers on a zone don't pop up correctly.	Not enough water pressure to run the zone. Main system shutoff valve is not fully open.	Split the zone in two. Open the system shutoff valve counterclockwise.
	Flow control on the zone valve is partially closed.	Open the flow control counterclockwise.
The sprinkler pops up, but no water sprays.	Radius adjustment screw may be turned fully off. Nozzle clogged by debris. Internal nozzle screen may be plugged by debris. Broken sprinkler.	Turn the screw counterclockwise. Remove and clean nozzle. Flush out nozzle screen. Replace the sprinkler.
A rotary sprinkler won't rotate.	Too little water pressure. Sprinkler is broken.	Increase water pressure. Replace the sprinkler.
There is a gap in the spray pattern.	Debris stuck in sprinkler nozzle and/or head. Sprinkler is faulty.	Clean out the sprinkler head and nozzle. Replace the sprinkler.
Sprinkler rotates in one direction, then stops.	Not enough pressure to rotate sprinkler. Faulty sprinkler head.	Increase the water pressure. Replace the sprinkler.
Water floods from a sprinkler.	Sprinkler nozzle missing. Cracked or missing sprinkler head.	Replace the missing nozzle. Replace the sprinkler.
A sprinkler will not retract after watering.	Debris is stuck between the sprinkler riser and the riser seal. Damaged riser or riser seal. Damaged retraction spring.	Remove any debris from the seal. Replace the seal or replace the sprinkler. Replace the sprinkler.

Water Supply Troubleshooting

Symptom	Cause	Solution
House water is contaminated with bacteria.	No backflow prevention on the system.	Install the mandated backflow prevention.
There is water runoff after a zone finishes watering.	System is overwatering. System is watering a slope.	Reduce the run times for the affected zones. Irrigate slopes for shorter periods but more often, or reduce the sprinkler precipitation rate for that zone.
Water is puddling in the yard.	Leak in the system. Punctured drip-irrigation line. System is irrigating too long.	Locate the leak and repair it, or replace the broken part. Use a hole plug to repair the leak. Reduce the minutes of run time for your zones.
There is no water in one part of one zone.	Poly supply line may be kinked. Rock or other debris is deforming the supply pipe. A buildup of debris and sediment has blocked the line.	Inspect the lines and straighten any kinks. Inspect the line, remove any rocks, and bed the pipe in sand. Flush out the zone lines thoroughly.
Freeze damage during winter occurred.	System was not properly stored for the winter.	Add drain valves at the lowest point in each zone; use compressed air to blow out system before winter; increase water pressure.

GLOSSARY

Adapter: A fitting that makes it possible to go from male endings to female endings or vice-versa. Transition adapters allow for joining different kinds of pipe together in the same run.

Backflow preventer: A device that protects the household water supply from the incursion of dirt, bacteria, pesticides, and other contaminants that can siphon into supply lines when an irrigation system is shut off. Backflow devices include vacuum breakers, double-check backflow preventers, and reduced-pressure backflow preventers.

Box: A metal or plastic container with openings for electrical cable. All electrical connections must be made inside a code-approved electrical box.

Bubbler: Sometimes known as a flood head, this head delivers a large quantity of water to a relatively small area. The coverage is typically no more than a circumference of 5 feet.

Buffalo box: A type of whole-house shutoff where the valve is in a plastic or concrete box set in the ground.

Circuit breaker: A protective device in a service panel that shuts off power to its circuit automatically when it senses a short circuit or overload.

Clay loam: A dense topsoil in which roots grow well; absorbs water slowly.

Common wire: The wire that brings power to the switch or to the fixture.

Compression fitting: A brass or plastic fitting used to join pipe by tightening two nuts that force a ring like ferrule into the fitting to assure a tight seal.

Coupling: A copper, galvanized-steel, plastic, or brass fitting used to connect two lengths of pipe.

Dielectric fitting: This fitting joins copper and steel pipe. By means of a specially designed plastic washer, it insulates the pipes from an otherwise corrosive chemical reaction.

Elbow: A fitting used to change the direction of a water line. Also known as an ell.

Emitters: Microirrigation watering heads including porous pipe, punch-in, in-line, and microsprinkler types.

Evapotranspiration: The measure of the amount of water that evaporates from the soil, plus the amount of water that is transpired by plants. The sum of the two is measured in inches or centimeters per day.

Fertigation: Adding fertilizer to a microirrigation system by means of an in-line applicator.

Fitting: Any connector (except a valve) that lets you join pipes of similar or dissimilar size or material in straight runs or at an angle.

Flow: A measurement in gallons per minute of the amount of water a water system can deliver. See also *Pressure gauge.*

Frost heave: The upthrust of soil caused when moist soil freezes. Supply lines that do not extend below the frost line are subject to frost heave.

Frost line: The maximum depth frost normally penetrates the soil during the winter. This depth varies from area to area depending on the climate.

Fuse: A safety device, located in an electrical fuse box, that shuts off power when a circuit overloads.

Gear-driven sprinkler: This pop-up rotary head includes a series of gears that drive the stream in a smooth and nearly noiseless pattern. See also *Pop-up spray head.*

Grease cap: A grease-filled, waterproof plastic protective cap that screws onto twisted-together wires to complete a splice.

Ground: Wire or metal sheathing that provides an alternate path for current back to the service panel (and from there to a grounding rod sunk in the earth, or to a cold-water pipe). Grounding protects against shock in case of an electrical malfunction.

Ground Fault Circuit Interrupter (GFCI): A receptacle with a built-in safety feature, which shuts off when there is a risk of shock.

Hardpan: A layer of rock or extremely compacted clay that is impervious to water and very difficult to dig through.

Hydrozoning: An irrigation layout that conserves water by using numerous irrigation zones to precisely deliver only the amount of water plant groupings require. Hydrozones typically serve specific plant types.

I.D.: The abbreviation for inside diameter. All plumbing pipes are sized according to their inside diameter. See also *O.D.*

Impact sprinkler: Also known as an impulse sprayer, this head uses a spring-loaded drive arm that, when pulled into the stream of water, is deflected sideways, giving a jerky rotational movement and a familiar sh-sh-sh sound. See also *Rotary head.*

Junction box: An electrical box with no fixture or device attached; it is used to split a circuit into different branches.

Manifold: A grouping of valves to one supply line. Manifolds can be made on site of PVC or purchased readymade.

Microclimate: A very localized weather condition, usually resulting from varying exposure to the sun or protection from wind. Several microclimates that are cooler, drier, or more humid than the prevailing weather can occur in a single yard.

Microirrigation: A low-pressure irrigation technology that uses a combination of drip and spray applicators to apply water directly to the root zone of plants. The feeder tubes and emitters are very small and can often be covered by mulch.

Multistream rotor: This head, used for irrigating turf and shrubs, produces several streams while rotating slowly.

Nipple: A 12-inch or shorter pipe with threads on both ends that is used to join fittings. A close nipple has threads that run from both ends to the center.

Nominal size: The designated dimension of a pipe or fitting. It varies slightly from the actual size.

O.D.: The abbreviation for outside diameter. See also *I.D.*

PE: Flexible PE (polyethylene) supply pipe is the newest type of plastic pipe. Many codes restrict its use.

Pipe-joint compound: A material applied to steel pipe threads to ensure a watertight or airtight seal. Also called pipe dope.

Pipe-thread tape: A synthetic pipe-thread wrapping that seals a joint in threaded steel or copper pipe.

Pop-up spray head: Generally set flush with the soil, these heads contain a stem that rises when the water is turned on to allow the spray to reach above nearby plants. See also *Gear-driven sprinkler.*

Pressure gauge: A device that can be attached to a home's water system to measure in pounds per square inch (P.S.I.) static water pressure. It is sometimes combined with a flow meter. See also *Static water pressure, flow.*

P.S.I.: The abbreviation for pounds per square inch. Water pressure is rated at so many P.S.I.

PVC: Polyvinylchloride (PVC) pipe is the most commonly accepted type of plastic drain pipe. PVC is sometimes also used for supply pipes in irrigation installations.

Reducer: A fitting with different size openings at either end used to go from a larger to a smaller pipe.

Riser: A vertical pipe supplying water to an irrigation spray head. In general plumbing parlance, a location or a supply tube running from a pipe to a sink or toilet.

Rotary head: Also known as stream heads, these heads cover the largest area of any head. They send out a high-velocity stream of water in one or two directions while rotating slowly in a sweep of up to 360 degrees. See also *Impact sprinkler.*

Sandy loam: A topsoil in which plant roots grow well but where watering is difficult because the soil drains quickly. This soil benefits from short, frequent waterings.

Service panel: A large electrical box, containing either fuses or circuit breakers. Power from the utility enters the service panel, where it is divided up into branch circuits. Also called a panel box or main panel.

Silt loam: A fairly fine-textured topsoil that holds minerals and water well. Most plants thrive in it. Only if clay predominates over sand in its composition will puddling be a problem.

Slope: A percentage derived from dividing the rise of an incline by its run. For example, the slope of an incline that rises 2 feet in a run of 12 feet would be calculated $2 \div 12 \times 100 = 16.66\%$.

Static water pressure: The water pressure available when no water is running inside or outside the house. See also *Pressure gauge.*

Stationary spray head: Because these heads do not rotate or pop up, they are the most maintenance-free type of spray head.

Stripping: Removing insulation from wire or sheathing from cable.

Sweating: A technique used to produce watertight joints between copper pipe and fittings. A pipe and fitting are cleaned, coated with flux, and pushed together. When the fitting is heated to the proper temperature with a torch, solder is drawn into the joint by capillary action to make the seal.

Tee: A T-shaped fitting used to tap into a length of pipe at a 90-degree angle for the purpose of beginning a branch line.

Timer: A device, also sometimes referred to as a controller, that switches on irrigation valves and lets them run for a preset time before switching them off.

Transition fitting: Any one of several fittings that joins pipe made of dissimilar materials, such as copper and plastic, plastic and cast iron, or galvanized steel and copper.

Union: A fitting used in runs of threaded pipe to facilitate adding a tee.

Wiper seal: A rubber or plastic gasket in pop-up spray heads that keeps dirt and debris out of the mechanism.

Xeriscaping: This landscaping practice encourages the use of native or well-adapted plants that are suited to the amount of precipitation available in a given region.

Zone: A section of an irrigation system that has a number of sprinkler devices sharing the same water lines and a common irrigation valve controlled independently by the irrigation timer. Also known as a circuit.

INDEX

Boldface numbers indicate pages with photographs or illustrations related to the topic.

METRIC CONVERSIONS

U.S. Units to Metric Equivalents			Metric Units to U.S. Equivalents		
To Convert From	Multiply By	To Get	To Convert From	Multiply By	To Get
Inches	25.4	Millimeters	Millimeters	0.0394	Inches
Inches	2.54	Centimeters	Centimeters	0.3937	Inches
Feet	30.48	Centimeters	Centimeters	0.0328	Feet
Feet	0.3048	Meters	Meters	3.2808	Feet
Yards	0.9144	Meters	Meters	1.0936	Yards
Square inches	6.4516	Square centimeters	Square centimeters	0.1550	Square inches
Square feet	0.0929	Square meters	Square meters	10.764	Square feet
Square yards	0.8361	Square meters	Square meters	1.1960	Square yards
Acres	0.4047	Hectares	Hectares	2.4711	Acres
Cubic inches	16.387	Cubic centimeters	Cubic centimeters	0.0610	Cubic inches
Cubic feet	0.0283	Cubic meters	Cubic meters	35.315	Cubic feet
Cubic feet	28.316	Liters	Liters	0.0353	Cubic feet
Cubic yards	0.7646	Cubic meters	Cubic meters	1.308	Cubic yards
Cubic yards	764.55	Liters	Liters	0.0013	Cubic yards

To convert from degrees Fahrenheit (F) to degrees Celsius (C), first subtract 32, then multiply by ⅝.

To convert from degrees Celsius to degrees Fahrenheit, multiply by ⅝, then add 32.

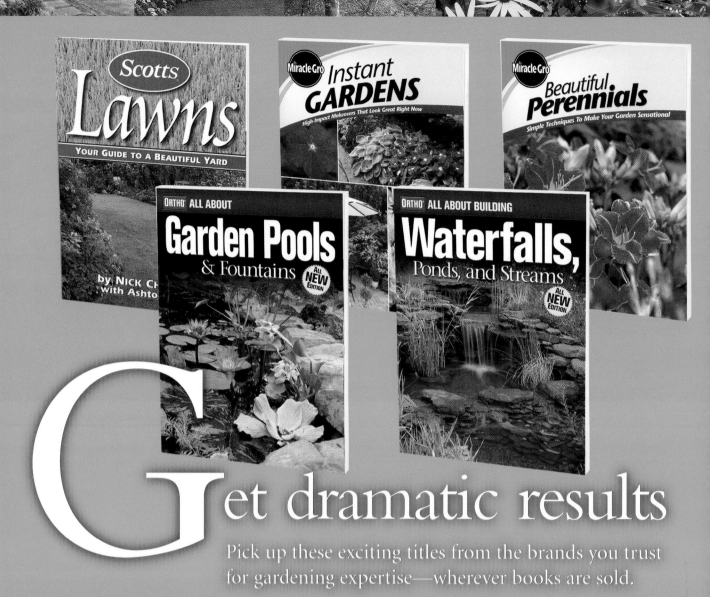